Volume 3

Published by CelebrityPress®, Orlando, FL.

CelebrityPress® is a registered trademark.

Printed in the United States of America.

ISBN: 978-1-7369881-6-9
LCCN: 2015941221

This publication is designed to provide accurate and authoritative information with regard to the subject matter covered. It is sold with the understanding that the publisher is not engaged in rendering legal, accounting, or other professional advice. If legal advice or other expert assistance is required, the services of a competent professional should be sought. The opinions expressed by the authors in this book are not endorsed by CelebrityPress® and are the sole responsibility of the author rendering the opinion.

Most CelebrityPress® titles are available at special quantity discounts for bulk purchases for sales promotions, premiums, fundraising, and educational use. Special versions or book excerpts can also be created to fit specific needs.

For more information, please write:
CelebrityPress®
3415 W. Lake Mary Blvd. #9550370
Lake Mary, FL 32746
or call 1.877.261.4930

Visit us online at: www.CelebrityPressPublishing.com

Volume 3

CelebrityPress®
Lake Mary, Florida

CONTENTS

CHAPTER 1

SUCCESS IS A MATTER OF FOCUS

BY JACK CANFIELD

Most people today believe they are entitled to a great life. They believe that—just because we exist—the Universe, the government, our employer, society, and countless other unseen benefactors are somehow "responsible" for delivering abundance, happiness, quality of life, vibrant health, exciting opportunities, acknowledgment by our peers, financial security, and other guarantees of success.

Of course, this sense of entitlement is a myth.

Because the fact is, there's only one person ultimately responsible for making sure you live the life you want.

That person is YOU.

When you take 100% responsibility for your outcomes in life, it means that—for better or worse—you are in control. You have unlimited power over what you can accomplish and over which challenges you'll persevere and conquer.

It also means that, if results don't turn out the way we expect, we should ask ourselves, *What else could I have done? Did I ask for the help I wanted and needed? Did I fail to fully explain the outcomes I wanted? What will I need to do differently the next time?* You soon realize that you can either actively create things in your life, or you can allow them to happen through sheer inaction—including creating or allowing things you may not like. To achieve the success you want, you must be willing to do things that are uncomfortable, say what's necessary, and take actions others may not support, like, or approve of.

In short, you get what *you* focus on.

DEFINE "SUCCESS" BY DECIDING WHAT YOU WANT

High achievers know what they want out of life—and they focus on achieving it. They take the time to decide what their income, relationships, finances, lifestyle, accomplishments, personal growth, recreation, contribution, and other lifestyle attributes will be.

If you aspire to join this elite group of purposeful individuals, there's a process I teach for deciding what you want—and for focusing on bringing good things into your life. It's called *The Vision Exercise*.

Begin by listening to some relaxing music and sitting quietly in a comfortable environment where you will not be interrupted. You can either audio-record the following instructions yourself, then play them back during the exercise, or you can have a friend slowly read the step-by-step instructions to you, pausing after each question and giving you time to allow the answers to become clear. At the end, be prepared to write down your answers in a journal for future reference.

Then, begin to visualize your ideal life *exactly the way you want it as if you are living it now.*

1. First, visualize your financial situation. What is your monthly or yearly income? How much money do you have in your savings? What is your net worth? How is your cash flow? Do you have all the financial advisors you want? A good accountant? An investment advisor? Next, what does your home look like? Where is it located? What does the interior look like? What color are the walls? How is it furnished? Are there paintings hanging in the rooms? What do they look like? Walk through your perfect house visually room by room, using your mind's eye to fill in all the details.

   At this point, don't worry about how you'll get that house. Don't sabotage yourself by saying, "I can't live in Malibu because I don't make enough money." Once you give your mind's eye the picture, your subconscious mind will solve the "not enough money" challenge.

   Simply be honest with yourself about what you truly want. Continue visualizing your perfect home. Next, visualize what kind of car you are driving, as well as any other possessions you'll now own because of your desired financial success.

2. Next, visualize your career. What are you doing in your career? Where are you working? With whom are you working? What does your workspace look like? What kind of clients do you have? What is your compensation like? Is it your own business? How many hours a week do you work?

3. Then, focus on your free time and recreation time. What are you doing with your family and friends in the free time you've created for yourself? What hobbies are you pursuing? What kinds of vacations do you take?

4. Next, visualize your body and your physical health, your emotional and spiritual life. Are you strong, flexible, fit, and healthy? Are you pain-free? Do you have trainers you work with or a health club you belong to? Are you free and open, relaxed, and in a state of peace, happiness, and joy all day

long? What does that look like? What is your spiritual life like?

5. Then move on to visualizing your relationships with your family and friends. What is your relationship with your family like? Who are your friends? What is the quality of your friendships? What do those friendships feel like? Are they loving, supportive, and empowering? Visualize them exactly the way you'd like them to be?

6. What about your own personal growth? Do you see yourself going back to school, taking trainings, seeking counseling, coaching or therapy for a past hurt, or a place where you feel stuck—or something else? Do you have a mentor?

7. Move on to the geographic community you live in or the wider community of people you've chosen to interact with. What does your ideal vision of that look like? What kinds of community activities are you involved in? What charities or nonprofits do you support? What do you do to help others and make a difference? How often every week do you participate in these activities? Who are you helping? Are you involved politically? If so, in what way?

To help you focus on bringing about this vision for your life, review your notes daily—visualizing what you'll be doing once your vision is achieved. What emotions will you feel? What are the sights and sounds you see? Is anyone else there congratulating you or enjoying the intended outcome with you?

FOCUS ON GOALS THAT WILL DELIVER YOUR VISION

It's not enough to just dream about what you want. You have to take steps to get there. But how do you know which steps to take? Here's how: turn your dreams into specific and measurable goals, and then take daily steps to reach those goals.

Extensive study has shown that when we focus on achieving specific goals, our subconscious mind actually helps us bring about those outcomes. In fact, when you give it a goal to work on, the mind will trigger the brain's *reticular activating system*—a web of neuropathways that sorts through the millions of random images, facts, and information we're bombarded with each day—and then sends to our conscious mind those information bits that will help us achieve our goals. When you give your brain an image of something you want to achieve (through visualizing that outcome), it will labor around the clock to find ways to achieve the picture you put there.

Without a doubt, the brain is a goal-seeking instrument.

How Much – By When?

In order for your brain to function optimally in helping you produce the results you want, it needs to know exactly what you want and by when you want it. When I teach about goal-setting in my live trainings, I stress the importance of setting goals that are measurable (how much) and time-specific (by when).

Measurable—The most powerful goals are those that are *measurable*, both by you and by others. Measurable means a numerical amount of dollars, square feet, acres, clients, Facebook followers, sales, impressions, books sold, podcast subscribers, 5-star reviews, etc. For instance, your goal might be to generate a specific number of new clients for your new consulting firm so you can meet your income goals and generate further referrals.

Time-specific—Your goal should also be *time-specific*. In other words, not only should you state *how much* you'll earn, but also *by when* you'll earn it. Only with both these units of measure in place can you determine whether you've achieved your final goal.

Additionally, when you decide on the model and color of the car you'll buy with your new-found income...the kind of house you'll

move into…which private schools your children will attend…
how you'll look and feel as a successful consultant…you can't
help but notice the positive emotions attached to those specific
images. When you add emotion, color, detail, and other features
to your goals, your brain will begin in earnest to seek out ways
to fulfill them. It will come up with creative ideas, recognize
opportunities and create positive motivation to take the necessary
actions.

CREATING A BREAKTHROUGH GOAL CAN UPLEVEL YOUR ENTIRE LIFE

Perhaps the true benefit of any goal is that—by pursuing it—you
become a more confident, competent person. No one can ever
take away the person you become as a result of pursuing your
loftiest goals.

In addition to your many weekly and monthly goals, I recommend
that you create *one single goal* such that, in the process of
achieving it, you uplevel every aspect of your life—from your
finances to your friends, your business success, your lifestyle,
and more. Wouldn't that be a goal you would want to work on
constantly and pursue with enthusiasm?

I call that a *Breakthrough Goal*—a goal that will quantum leap
your life.

For instance, if you were a teacher and you knew that you could
get promoted to school principal once you got your advanced
degree, wouldn't you work night and day to achieve that goal?

And if you developed a new learning modality, wrote a book
about it, started lecturing at education conferences, and
consulted with school districts across the country, wouldn't
that be something that would not only improve your career
prospects but also bring you a secondary income from your
teaching career?

16

That's an example of a breakthrough goal. Other examples include writing a book, developing an online program or an app to sell, getting your MBA degree, getting your realtors license, doubling your income, having a 5-minute drivetime radio show, opening up India or China as a market for your products, doubling your real estate portfolio, starting your own business, and learning another language so that you can do business in other countries.

FOCUS EVERY DAY BY PRACTICING THE RULE OF 5

In the world today, most people are rewarded for action, not for ideas. Yet it's surprising how many people get caught up in planning, deciding, investigating, and other preliminary activities—when what they should really be doing is simply taking action on their goals. When you take action, the Universe rewards that action with additional help that can speed you on your way. You also start to get useful feedback about your chosen path or methods.

THE WORLD DOESN'T PAY YOU FOR WHAT YOU KNOW — IT PAYS YOU FOR WHAT YOU DO

Many people have had good ideas—some of which led to entirely new industries or never-before-seen ways of making money. The Internet in its infancy was a place where many people had good ideas. But how many of those people took action and created the Googles, Yahoos, Amazons, and other businesses we know today?

The fact is that, while most people know *a lot* about making money or getting results or creating advancement in the world, very few actually get to *enjoy the rewards* of having this knowledge (whether the rewards are financial, professional, or congratulatory) simply because they are not among those select few who take sustained action.

Successful people, on the other hand, have a bias for *action*. More than any other characteristic, *action* is what separates the successful from the unsuccessful...the people who actually reap the rewards from those who would merely like to.

Perhaps you, too, had a great idea at one time—only to see it turned into a successful business or a new invention or a popular product *by someone else*—because they took action, and you did not.

The reality is that, in the world today, the people who are rewarded are those who take action. We're paid for what we do.

PRACTICE THE RULE OF 5

When *Chicken Soup for the Soul*® was first published, everyone on the team wanted it to become a *New York Times* #1 Bestseller. With that goal in mind, we interviewed dozens of book-marketing experts and sought the advice of numerous bestselling authors. We even read a book called *1001 Ways to Market Your Book* by John Kremer. And with literally thousands of strategies we could pursue, to be honest, achieving our goal of being a #1 NYT Bestseller began to seem a little overwhelming.

Then one day, we were talking to a friend who reminded us that even the largest tree could be felled simply by swinging an ax at its trunk just five times a day. "Eventually," he concluded, "the tree will have to come down, no matter how large."

Out of that advice, we developed The Rule of 5: accomplishing five simple things every day that will move you closer to completing your goal.

In the case of *Chicken Soup for the Soul*, it meant doing five radio interviews a day. Or sending out five review copies to newspapers every day. Or asking five pastors to use a story from the book in their sermons. Or calling five companies to buy a copy for all their workers. Or sending five press releases a day. And on and on...every day for more than two years. Not only was it worth it, but the original *Chicken Soup for the Soul* book did go on to reach #1 on *The New York Times* and *USA Today* bestseller lists—and it has also sold more than 11 million copies in 41 languages worldwide.

What could you do in your life if you chose a breakthrough goal, then did five things every day to bring you closer to achieving it?

FOCUS ON YOUR LIFE PURPOSE

In closing, while it's important to take 100% responsibility, set goals, and stay in action, all your goal-setting and action plans may not ultimately be fulfilling for you if they are not directed toward a purpose that you're passionate about. As Steven Covey so eloquently put it, *You don't want to get to the top of the ladder only to find that you've had it leaning against the wrong wall.*

If your breakthrough goals are not aligned with your Life Purpose, you could find yourself achieving it, but not really being satisfied or feeling fulfilled. We all know of wealthy, famous people who are not happy—maybe even drug or alcohol-addicted and suicidal.

I discovered my life purpose many decades ago. It is "to inspire and empower people to live their highest vision in a context of love and joy in harmony with the highest good of all concerned."

Through my many books, the *Chicken Soup for the Soul* series, my trainings and packaged courses, I've made it my life's work to inspire and empower people. And every day that I do this work, I feel that I'm in my right livelihood. Purpose has brought a sense of deep fulfillment to my life.

But without a clear sense of purpose, it's easy for you to get sidetracked and lose focus. Discovering your life purpose, on the other hand, means you can organize all your activities around it. If a certain opportunity, project, or activity doesn't align with your purpose, you choose not to work on it. Period. Not only is this kind of focus a relief (because you don't have to do everything that comes your way), but it's also incredibly liberating to know you can say "no" with conviction—and confidence—that the *right opportunities* are just around the corner, waiting for you to make space in your life.

True success in life is joyfully pursuing what you are programmed for and destined to do. Take the time to discover your purpose, follow your heart, clarify the vision that will fulfill that purpose, turn your vision into goals, focus on those goals every day by practicing the rule of 5, make corrections based on the feedback you get along the way, and never give up on fulfilling your vision.

And remember, success really is a matter of focus.

About Jack

Known as America's #1 Success Coach, Jack Canfield is the CEO of the Canfield Training Group in Santa Barbara, CA, which trains and coaches entrepreneurs, corporate leaders, managers, sales professionals, and the general public in how to accelerate the achievement of their personal, professional, and financial goals.

Jack Canfield is best known as the co-author of the #1 New York Times bestselling *Chicken Soup for the Soul®* book series, which has sold more than 500 million books in 49 languages, including 11 New York Times #1 bestsellers. As the CEO of Chicken Soup for the Soul Enterprises, he helped grow the *Chicken Soup for the Soul®* brand into a virtual empire of books, children's books, audios, videos, CDs, classroom materials, a syndicated column, and a television show, as well as a vigorous program of licensed products that includes everything from clothing and board games to nutraceuticals and a successful line of Chicken Soup for the Pet Lover's Soul® cat and dog foods.

His other books include *The Success Principles™: How to Get from Where You Are to Where You Want to Be* (now available in its 10th Anniversary Edition), *The Success Principles for Teens, The Aladdin Factor, Dare to Win, Heart at Work, The Power of Focus: How to Hit Your Personal, Financial and Business Goals with Absolute Certainty, You've Got to Read This Book, Tapping into Ultimate Success, Jack Canfield's Key to Living the Law of Attraction,* his recent novel, *The Golden Motorcycle Gang: A Story of Transformation* and *The 30-Day Sobriety Solution.*

Jack is a dynamic speaker and was inducted into the National Speakers Association's Speakers Hall of Fame. He has appeared on more than 1,000 radio and television shows, including *Oprah, Montel, Larry King Live,* the *Today Show, Fox and Friends,* and two hour-long PBS Specials devoted exclusively to his work. Jack is also a featured teacher in 12 movies, including *The Secret, The Meta-Secret, The Truth, The Keeper of the Keys, Tapping into the Source,* and *The Tapping Solution.* Jack was also honored with a documentary produced about his life and teachings called *"The Soul of Success: The Jack Canfield Story."*

Jack has personally helped hundreds of thousands of people on six different continents become multi-millionaires, business leaders, best-selling authors, leading sales professionals, successful entrepreneurs, and world-class athletes while at the same time creating balanced, fulfilling, and healthy lives.

His corporate clients have included Virgin Records, SONY Pictures, Daimler-Chrysler, Federal Express, GE, Johnson & Johnson, Merrill Lynch, Campbell's Soup, Re/Max, The Million Dollar Forum, The Million Dollar Roundtable, The Young Entrepreneurs Organization, The Young Presidents Organization, the Executive Committee, and the World Business Council.

He is the founder of the Transformational Leadership Council and a member of Evolutionary Leaders, two groups devoted to helping create a world that works for everyone.

Jack is a graduate of Harvard, earned his M.Ed. from the University of Massachusetts, and has received three honorary doctorates in psychology and public service. He is married, has three children, two stepchildren, and a grandson.

For more information, visit:
- www.JackCanfield.com or www.CanfieldTraintheTrainer.com.

CHAPTER 2

LOVE NEVER FAILS

BY MICHAEL REZA

When I first began contemplating the chapter for this book – the essence, the very *soul of success* – my thoughts instantly went to 1 Corinthians: 13. I remembered being asked on two separate occasions to read this most well-known passage at my brother's as well as at my sister's weddings years ago:

Love is patient, love is kind. It does not envy, it does not boast, it is not proud. It does not dishonor others, it is not self-seeking, it is not easily angered, it keeps no record of wrongs.

Most people are familiar with this passage, and it is commonly associated with romantic love and is frequently read at weddings. But, when I read it at my sister's wedding, it struck me rather profoundly that the very essence of the entirety of 1 Corinthians: 13 is not about romantic love. It is about Agape, a self-giving love that gives without demanding or expecting repayment. This is the love my mother taught and talked about in our family as she raised me and my seven siblings. Mom taught us that there are many kinds of love. Specifically, there are four kinds of love mentioned in the bible. But Agape, which is the fourth kind of love, is what she spoke of frequently and was most intent on establishing the importance of this one in our young hearts.

Since my sister's wedding, 1 Corinthians: 13 has been a daily part of my life. I read it almost every morning, and I do my best to practice Agape in all of my day-to-day affairs. I am certain that the successes I've experienced throughout my life are a result of the solid, unshakeable foundation of unconditional love my parents provided and the importance they placed on the power of Agape love.

SUCCESS IS PROMISED

We've all heard it thousands of times: *All you need is love.* But how sincerely do we contemplate that statement? How intently do we determine to make love the guiding factor in our everyday lives and businesses? How consciously do we practice love with our co-workers, employees, friends, acquaintances, and the strangers we meet and interact with? Until I read 1 Corinthians: 13 at my sister's wedding, my life was without question wonderful. I had been weaned on kindness and unconditional love, and everything I did was based on goodness. However, when I began to consciously read and consciously observe my thoughts, words, and actions from the perspective of Agape, the miracles have been non-stop. The successes have been beyond my wildest dreams.

The promise of 1 Corinthians: 13 is that *Love never fails.* This is a very succinct promise. Even though it was written in the third century, its message is as relevant and perhaps more so today. As a young man, I took this promise to heart. Early in my professional life, I placed all of my eggs in that basket and placed all of my bets on that one promise. With each passing year, the more I studied this bible passage, the more I could see what each of its stanzas referred to in everyday life. I could see the lack of understanding and love in the behavior and hearts of others with whom I came into contact. If my words and or actions could influence even a momentary respite from the suffering caused by confusion – and I could never know for certain if it did – then it was my pleasure to offer kind and loving words in every situation.

If I speak in the tongues of men or of angels, but do not have love,
I am only a resounding gong or a clanging cymbal.
~ 1 Corinthians: 13

This passage of 1 Corinthians: 13 reminds me of the Enron scandal that happened back in 2006. The Enron executives assured their employees and shareholders that nothing was wrong and that all was well with the company. But we all know that was not the case. Shareholders in the company lost $74 billion, and the employees who put their retirement money into Enron stock also lost billions. And all 5,000 employees lost their jobs. This is a perfect example of "speaking in the tongues of men or of angels without love." Perhaps you can think of experiences closer to home and less devastating that also exemplify the meaning of this passage. I've heard parents talk about telling their kids to "do as I say, not as I do." That's a classic example. As human beings, there have been times when we have all been guilty of being a "resounding gong or clanging cymbal."

When I began my conscientious studies of 1 Corinthians: 13, I had already experienced what I consider to be some degree of success. However, as my understanding grew, I began to examine my thoughts about success more deeply. I wondered about its true meaning. Success is commonly defined as "attaining wealth, prosperity and/or fame."

Of course, I had dreams and I wanted nice things. I wanted a family for whom I could provide a lovely home, a good education, and the good things in life. I wanted to travel and see the world. I wanted to enjoy life's luxuries. But there was a deeper question that kept coming up. Why, I wondered, do so many people have an overwhelming desire to strive for wealth and fame? Why are so many people willing to hurt others to attain wealth and fame? When the answer came to me, it was eye-opening. It occurred to me that many people pursue success so that others will love them. Or so they can think of themselves as being worthy of love. Ultimately, all the striving for success is just another way that we are all looking for love.

It may be difficult to understand how the Enron executives were looking for love. Or another example on a massively catastrophic level is that of Bernie Madoff, who bilked his clients out of billions of dollars. He talked a good game, but none of it meant anything. It was all self-serving. There was no love motivating the actions of the Enron executives or Bernie Madoff.

Fortunately, there are even more examples of business owners and leaders who care about their employees and shareholders. These are the people to emulate. We sold our company to Berkshire Hathaway, owned by Warren Buffet, who I consider a man of the highest integrity. In an interview I once saw him give, he mentioned that he only buys companies from owners who love their businesses and treat their employees with love. Mr. Buffet made a "Giving Pledge" that goes like this: "More than 99% of my wealth will go to philanthropy during my lifetime or at death." He goes on to say that "Were my family to use more than 1% of my Berkshire Hathaway stock certificates on ourselves, neither our happiness nor our well-being would be enhanced. In contrast, that remaining 99% can have a huge effect on the health and welfare of others." That is not the cacophony of a resounding gong or clanging cymbal, but the sound of love and caring for others.

Another example of love comes from a friend of mine from high school. Doug LaBouff started a Friends-to-Friends club to have students help students in need. He then later joined the military to serve our country, during which he made the ultimate sacrifice, leaving behind a wife and children he loved.

It is important to base our dreams and aspirations on love in service to humanity.

If I have the gift of prophecy and can fathom all mysteries and
all knowledge, and if I have a faith that can move mountains,
but do not have love, I am nothing.
~ 1 Corinthians: 13

To a significant number of people, wealth and fame are synonymous with power. To these people, power is what makes them feel worthy. This happens in every profession, from law enforcement and education to religion and politics, small businesses, and international corporations. We have seen the abuse of power most frequently in the summer of 2020. We have seen it in religious organizations and in the film industry, which gave rise to the "Me Too" movement. When 1 Corinthians: 13 was written by the apostle Paul, he was very clear in expressing that any activity performed without love is meaningless. The pursuit of power for power's sake is ultimately meaningless. It is just another way some people attempt to find love or feel worthy of love. Falls from positions of perceived power are often very public and destroy lives, not just the life of the person who abused their power, but their families and associates. It doesn't matter how smart you are, how far-reaching your knowledge extends, or how deep your faith is in yourself; if you do not have love for humanity, it is all meaningless.

What so many people still do not understand is that love is within us. Love is all around us. It is a gift that has been freely given to us and is our gift to give without expecting anything in return.

If I give all I possess to the poor and give over my body to hardship that I may boast, but do not have love, I gain nothing.
~ 1 Corinthians: 13

Have you heard anyone talk about how much money they give to charities each year? Or how much time they spend volunteering, so much so that they don't have time to spend with their friends or families? Or how brilliant they are or how well-travelled they are? Have you heard anyone actually profess to having earned "bragging rights?"

We were taught as children not to boast or brag or talk about ourselves. Boasting is defined as speaking "with exaggeration and excessive pride, especially about oneself." I'm sure you can think of examples in your own life, perhaps among co-workers or bosses, or people you don't know. Once you become attuned to these passages from 1 Corinthians: 13, you will be able to recognize that there is no love in boasting or bragging. It is a completely self-serving act. Again, it is a way humans have of making themselves feel important, a way of looking for love.

I often think about the lesson of the widow's mite presented in the Synoptic Gospels, in which Jesus is teaching at the Temple in Jerusalem. According to the Gospel of Mark, the widow gave two mites, which, when put together, are worth a quadrans, the smallest Roman coin. It doesn't matter how much you give. As Warren Buffet pointed out in his Giving Pledge, those who give the least sacrifice the most, because they are giving their all, while the wealthy may give a lot, but it doesn't affect their lives. I have seen this time and time again when I was on the Board of the Congressional Awards program, which recognizes young people for their voluntary public service. During thousands of hours in service, I have seen ordinary people performing extraordinary acts of love and kindness. I watched an 18-year-old burn victim spend hundreds of hours in the hospital helping other burn victims. Each and every one of us has a purpose to serve others in love. It is an infallible method for success.

In these contemporary times in which we live, social media provides new platforms for people who love to boast. People who are secure in their abilities and integrity do not talk about themselves. And let me clarify one point. Make no mistake that experiencing a feeling of self-respect and personal worth or satisfaction with your achievements is a crucial part of healthy self-esteem. It is when you boast or brag to others, full of exaggerated pride, that gains you nothing.

Consider Mother Teresa, known for giving her all to help feed the poor and spread the good news, often risking her own life for her missionary work. My mother and so many mothers and fathers push through enormous challenges, working in every way to give

28

their loved ones more than they had, at times sacrificing their own health and well-being for the well-being of their children.

Love does not delight in evil but rejoices with the truth.
It always protects, always trusts, always hopes, always perseveres.
~ 1 Corinthians: 13

I have heard parents talk about how they have to "toughen" their kids up so that they'll be able to handle life. I've also heard people in corporate settings talk about having to be "tough" so they are not taken advantage of in business. Whenever I hear this, it makes me sad. I'm sad for the child and for the parent. I'm sad for the person who is afraid of being taken advantage of.

I'm certain the parent thinks being tough on their kid is an act of love. But the child has no idea why they would need to be tough to face the world. Children come into this world innocent. It is our job as parents to protect them from harm, not to inflict harm upon them. It is the job of parents to trust that their child is here for a reason. It is a parent's job to tell the child the truth and to teach the child to tell the truth.

Whether you have children or not, whether you are a business owner or not, you are a human being, and you have dreams and aspirations. Perhaps you dream of having children someday or owning your own business, or both. If you set your sights on cultivating Agape love in your heart and your daily affairs and letting this love be your guide, I have no doubt that you will achieve your dreams and enjoy a sense of satisfaction and fulfillment. As this final passage from 1 Corinthians: 13 says, *love always perseveres, is always hopeful and rejoices with the truth.* I can assure you that I have been presented with opportunities and have enjoyed successes I could never have dreamed of since I decided to study and live according to Agape love as expressed in 1 Corinthians: 13.

Agape love has its place in every profession, every home, and every business setting. Instead of feeling you have to be tough to make it in the competitive business world, you could practice being more loving instead. Coming from a place of love has an effect on the people around you. People respond more favorably to kindness than to meanness or toughness.

Agape love is so great that it can be given to those who may be perceived as unlovable or unappealing. It is love that loves even when it is rejected. Agape love gives. It loves because it wants to; it does not demand or expect repayment from the love given. It gives because it loves; it does not love in order to receive.

If you dream of being successful, I encourage you to study and cultivate Agape love and let that love guide you in all of your affairs. If you have love in your heart, you are already a success.

Remember:

Love never fails.
~ 1 Corinthians: 13

About Michael

Distinguished in several professional arenas, Michael Reza's name is synonymous with fair lending practices in the financial industry, fair representation of his constituents in politics, as the long-term Congressional Awards President and Board Member, and as an Executive Producer in the film industry. He also actively participates in service to others through raising funds and awareness for a variety of organizations devoted to cancer research, youth, and HRH Prince Phillip Duke of Edinburgh's Award.

While serving on Fannie Mae's Advisory Board, Michael became the first lender entrusted to secure and issue mortgage-backed securities to Native Americans in the U.S.A. Michael has backed more than $50M worth of loans to this previously ignored population. Subsequently, through active participation in the first tax credit to Native Americans in the US, and after the sale of the tax credit, he went on to slash loan amounts and payments by 50%.

Michael was the President of the 34th Congressional District appointed by the local Congressman Esteban Torres. He was then appointed and confirmed to the Board of Directors of the Congressional Awards Board in 1993, for which Congress had to vet and vote him onto the Board. He was unanimously confirmed and approved by both, and he served in that role through 2003.

[N.B. The Congressional Award is the highest award given to youth in the U.S.A., and it was voted into Public Law 96-114.]

In his early years in the financial industry, after earning his MBA, Michael started a mortgage company which he led for 20 years before selling it to a public company. He then started another mortgage banking division which was subsequently sold to HomeServices of America, a Berkshire Hathaway Affiliate recognized as the largest, full-service independent residential real estate brokerage firm and the largest brokerage-owned settlement services (mortgage, title, escrow, and insurance) provider in the United States.

As the CEO and an owner of MCapital, Michael continues to build and cultivate long-term quality relationships by consistently providing exceptional customer service. He currently sits as an advisor or board member on over 25 companies from banks to non-profits, and serves as Executive Producer on the TV show, It's Happening Right Here.

Michael is expanding his reach into new territory as co-author of *Cracking The Success Code - Vol. 2*, with Brian Tracy, and *The Soul of Success - Vol. 3*, co-authored with Jack Canfield. All proceeds from these books are being donated to a variety of causes, including non-profits that are leading the way to bring an end to human trafficking, among others.

Michael lives in Southern California with his wife and their three teenage children, and his oldest son, Miles Reza, lives in Florida.

Contact information:
• www.Michaelareza.com

CHAPTER 3

HOW WE MAKE DECISIONS UNDER STRESS AND HOW WE CAN GET BETTER AT IT

BY DR. MARTHA BATORSKI

In 1937, Napoleon Hill published his study of over 500 self-made millionaires, including Andrew Carnegie, Henry Ford and Charles M. Schwab, in *Think and Grow Rich* (Hill, 2018). With over 15 million copies sold, this classic textbook has become a foundational text for understanding how successful people think.

Today's world differs significantly from the time of Carnegie, Ford, and Schwab. Our present time in history is characterized by faster rates of change, greater uncertainty, and relentless pressures. While the principles underlying successful thinking documented by Hill remain unchanged, our present-day realities require a deeper understanding of how successful people think *under stress.*

This chapter addresses this very subject, and is excerpted from a doctoral dissertation exploring the topic of judgment and decision making under stress and how we can get better at it (Batorski, 2011).

The study was inspired by a real-world problem I kept running into in my 30-year career as a management consultant. While helping organizations successfully implement largescale, transformational change over time, I repeatedly noticed a phenomenon of impaired judgment and decision making under stress in a large percentage of leaders overseeing the implementation of enterprise-wide change. This chapter sheds light on how common the phenomenon is, and how to address the growing need for better decision making in times of uncertainty.

Transformational change is not the easy-to-manage kind of change, but the deeply *stressful* kind. It is the kind of change that incapacitates, holds the brain hostage, and freezes the strongest among us. Transformational change (also known as deep change or *gamma* change) affects every aspect of an organization from people's jobs, roles, skills, technology, measures, strategy, business processes, and – most challenging of all – changes underlying what the organization holds to be important (culture). Unlike incremental change, deep change requires significant shifts from the status quo, accompanied by time pressure. My experience with 15+ largescale change initiatives showed a pattern of impaired decision making under stress in leaders, many of whom became overwhelmed and less than successful.

For individuals tasked with implementing largescale change, the impact of judgment errors (at a time when their leadership is most needed) can have disastrous consequences, including scuttled transformational change projects (at enormous cost), loss of trust in leadership by employees counting on them to bring about desired change (dashed hopes), and loss of positioning within an organization's industry due when they fail to adapt. There is a dearth of information to prepare successful leaders in the ability to lead change *and* the impact of how the brain reacts under stress. There is even less information available on effective techniques for developing a leader's resilience to stress.

When I took on the task of finding out what was happening in my clients' leadership teams to prepare leaders for decision making under stress, I did not know that there were two areas of study – Human Factors and Naturalistic Decision Making – that have focused for years on how people think in real world, dynamic settings with high uncertainty, incomplete information and high stakes for poor judgment calls gone awry. What I discovered in researching for my study was extremely useful information and worthy of a wider audience. To this day, when I present at medical schools, nursing schools, and health science universities, professionals are hearing about the mechanics of decision making under stress as if for the first time. Today's decision makers (you included) require more and deserve better. This chapter addresses these areas:

a) how successful people make decisions.
b) what specifically impairs judgment and decision making.
c) commonly used techniques to improve judgment and decision making under stress.
d) uncommon yet well-researched techniques for improving one's capacity for improved judgment and decision making under stress – the development of consciousness.

References are provided along the way for you to learn more on your own.

HOW WE MAKE DECISIONS IN DYNAMIC SETTINGS

Decision making under stress has been studied as far back as World War I and is referenced in military theory, law enforcement, aviation and aerospace, healthcare, firefighting, self-defense, and even sports. And a key concept in the study of judgment and decision making is called situation awareness (SA). This concept underlies all judgment and decision making in real-time. *Situation awareness is defined as the ability to know what is going on around you so that you know what to do,* and it involves three rapid-fire processes that precede the moment of decision making and subsequent actions that follow (Endsley,

1995). Figure 1.0 illustrates the elements: the first step is to take in information cues from the surroundings (*perception*), followed by attempts to make sense of what is being perceived (*comprehension*), followed by a rapid determination of what will likely happen next (*projection*). What follows then is the point of *decision*, and then *action*.

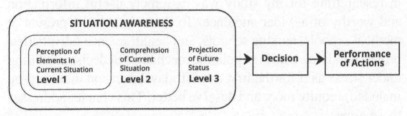

Figure 1.0 – Endsley, M. (1995). (Reprinted with permission of SAGE Publications.)

Here is an applied example of real-time judgment and decision making in a dynamic setting:

A hockey player surveys the ice for other players around the puck (perception). The player uses a real-time internal map of the position of players to make sense of what is happening relative to the zones on the ice (comprehension) and then rapidly judges where the puck will go (projection). A split-second decision is then made, followed by action. Take a moment to translate these three elements to a situation where you make real-time, dynamic decisions. These situations abound in daily life depending on one's profession (averting a potential driving incident, real-time problem solving in an operating room triage event, etc.).

WHAT IMPAIRS JUDGMENT AND DYNAMIC DECISION MAKING

There are thousands of cases of impaired situation awareness in the naturalistic decision making research that have resulted in errors leading to tragic outcomes and even loss of life.

Here are some examples from the world of sports and firefighting where advanced knowledge of impaired situation awareness prevented potential tragedies.

- An aerial gymnast notices that her internal tracking ability (perception, comprehension, projection) of her position in the air is "off" – i.e., she cannot tell where she is in her rotations relative to her landing spot. To avoid injury, she withdraws from the competition. (In sports, this impaired situation awareness is referred to as "the twisties.")
- Wildland firefighters on the fire line start exhibiting loss of judgment under the fatigue of long hours as well as the stress of a constantly changing environment (wind and humidity conditions). Those trained on the fire line to spot this condition remove those affected (this impaired situation awareness in firefighting is referred to as "retreating to the tailboard"). Firefighters are trained extensively in impaired situation awareness to prevent judgment errors that can result in potential loss of life.

By now you are hopefully seeing the pattern that I experienced on my transformational change projects: the leaders charged with transformational change initiatives would likely have had a fighting chance of success had they been armed with knowledge about the nature of change, the impact of stress on their own situation awareness, and the impact of impaired situation awareness on their own judgment and decision making.

Here is an abbreviated list of elements identified in the research (and examples from everyday situations to better recognize each one).

1. *Attentional tunneling* is a tendency to see an increasingly narrow portion of one's environment by locking on to certain aspects of the environment to the exclusion of the big picture. Example: a person learning a new area of specialization leaving out key steps as they master the material.
2. *Regression* is a tendency to revert under stress to earlier learned routines, even if not entirely appropriate to the

current situation. Example: a leader placed in an unfamiliar role as change agent operating outside their level of expertise retreats to their office, abdicating the urgent, complex issues to focus on tasks they know.

3. *Finite memory limitation* is the tendency to overload short-term memory with too much information. Example: a person asks for directions and becomes overwhelmed after receiving too much information from a local giving detailed directions.

4. *Workload, Anxiety, Fatigue, and Other Stressors (WAFOS)* is the tendency of an individual to degrade their situation awareness due to overexertion, working outside of one's level of expertise (anxiety-producing), and insufficient rest. Example: job burnout in front-line health workers addressing patients' needs in an overwhelmed hospital system.

5. *Complexity creep* is a tendency of the decision maker to incorrectly form sufficient internal representations of the big picture due to feature escalation. Example: confusion created by adding too many actions to a project plan rendering it unmanageable.

6. *Errant mental models* is a tendency to build a "false" (errant) internal "map" of a developing situation, making it difficult for a decision maker to detect cues and explain away conflicting cues to fit the mental model they have selected. Example: a heated argument ensues during a global pandemic on behaviors that will reduce illness and deaths. Depending on one's mental model, a decision is made on whether to comply with guidelines. An errant mental model gives greater credence to information that aligns only with beliefs while ignoring information that doesn't fit with those beliefs.

IMPAIRED JUDGMENT AND YOUR BRAIN

When conditions of urgency and high pressure take over, here is what happens next in the brain leading to impaired situation awareness:

1. The brain responds to stressful stimuli by sending a signal to the thalamus (which acts as the air traffic controller).
2. The thalamus sends information to the part of the brain just behind the forehead called the prefrontal cortex (CEO of the brain), as well as the amygdala (the emotional center of the brain that responds quickly to incoming stimuli).
3. The initial release of neurotransmitters and hormones into the brain continues to rapidly affect the prefrontal cortex and the amygdala. An overload of stress turns off the prefrontal cortex, resulting in a drop in IQ and ability to control the amygdala.
4. Simultaneously, increased stress turns on the amygdala creating an overly sensitive, heightened state of emotion. We experience this as a significant inability to control emotions, thus becoming not only temporarily impaired cognitively but also less emotionally intelligent.

When the brain becomes overwhelmed by the effects of the factors that impair judgment, there is an acute prefrontal shut down (the "dumbing down" effect). This results in a rapid decline in judgment due to the "fight or flight" response, releasing adrenalin and noradrenalin hormones in amounts so high that they cause certain neurological pathways in the brain to short-circuit. This short-circuiting functionally interferes with the biological processes involved in effective judgement and decision making when increasing demands, mounting pressure, and urgency overwhelm the brain's cognitive resources.

IMPROVING JUDGMENT AND DECISION-MAKING UNDER STRESS

Researchers in Human Factors and Naturalistic Decision Making have also identified many factors that improve situation awareness so the decision maker can improve the process of judgment and decision making. You will be able to relate to these valuable factors as well. Here is an abbreviated summary:

1) *Social factors (Sandoval, 2005):* values, norms, and beliefs have been shown to impact a person's ability to "see" cues (perception), make sense of the information (comprehension), and project where a situation is going before they decide and act. Example: nurses encouraged to speak up in a hospital setting show a dramatic decrease in errors (vs. hospital cultures where individuals face reprimands for speaking up due to hierarchical norms and structures).

2) *Individual factors (Endsley, 1995):* situation awareness has been shown to improve with these factors:

   a. *Cognitive maps and mental models*: the individual's beliefs create neural brain circuitry impacting what they can see, process, and assess. Example: Growth mindset ("I am a good problem-solver") vs. limiting mindset ("I am terrible at problem-solving").

   b. *Memory and automaticity*: memory recognition from repetition and previous experiences. Example: an experienced firefighter approaching a floor of a burning structure triggers a muscle memory recognition (perception of cues from the texture and "give" of the floor), creating instantaneous comprehension and projection that it is unsafe to proceed.

   c. *Abilities, experiences, training, and personality*: memory recognition built up over time from previous experiences build a resource from which to draw in like circumstances. Example: Just-In-Time training to reinforce skills by incorporating experience, training, assessment of skill level, and self-awareness of personality preferences to improve effectiveness.

d. *Goals, objectives, and preconceptions*: clarity created by goals (especially written), objectives, and positive expectations. Example: goals, objectives, and expectations focus the individual's awareness and weed out extraneous distractions from unprioritized choices.

These frameworks have explored the descriptive factors of how decision-making works in dynamic settings. However, few prescriptive studies exist that address ways to develop situation awareness capacity.

THE NEW FRONTIER: IMPROVING SITUATION AWARENESS CAPACITY THROUGH DEVELOPMENT OF CONSCIOUSNESS

My doctoral research addressed the absence of prescriptive studies in the literature on how to development situation awareness capacity to improve judgment and decision making under stress. My study explored whether the development of consciousness – inner restful alertness at the basis of situation awareness – might measurably improve the three areas of situation awareness using an easily learned and effortless meditation technique from the Vedic tradition. See Figure 2.0.

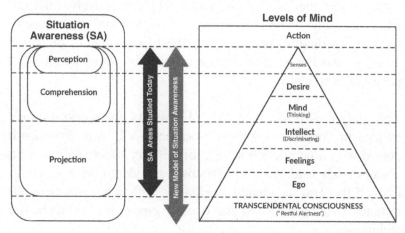

Figure 2.0

41

The ancient Vedic texts describe the distinct levels of the mind, which happen to map to the widely-used model of situation awareness. I re-oriented the SA model vertically to help the reader see the common areas of overlap. Note that the Vedic model of the mind adds the missing element of "restful alertness" or "transcendental consciousness." This was the variable I incorporated into the study using the Transcendental Meditation™ technique, chosen for the extensive research studies on its demonstrated efficacy in developing restful alertness. (There are more than 380 peer-reviewed research studies on the TM technique published in over 160 scientific journals. Many of the studies have been conducted at US and international universities and research centers, including Harvard, Stanford Medical School, Yale Medical School and UCLA Medical School).

There are many types of meditation practice. The criteria for the meditation practice I selected were that the subjects were able to easily learn how to access their inner state of restful alertness, that the subjects were able to automatically transcend the technique, and that the EEG signature of the technique was in the Alpha 1 range: 8-10 Hz. Travis and Shear (2008) compare the EEG signatures of many meditation techniques, grouping the categories of contemplation (open monitoring), concentration (focused attention), and automatic transcending. In this study each of the meditation categories had distinctively different EEG signatures. The Transcendental Meditation™ technique is the only meditation practice with the EEG signature of Alpha 1 range, and the meditation practice I know most about from personal experience.

The study took place at Norwich University, the oldest military college in the US (located in Northfield, VT) over a 3-month period with a population sample of military cadets and civilian leaders – all students. Two groups were identified: one group learned the Transcendental Meditation technique (practiced 20 minutes twice daily) and the control group did not learn the technique.

We all know the positive impact of a good night's sleep in improving one's ability to appreciate more from our surroundings (perception), make sense of problems faster (comprehension), and sense solutions more rapidly (projection). The study explored whether regular Transcendental Meditation practice resulted in a measurable change in the three elements of situation awareness in the demanding environment of student leaders.

Results: pre- and post-study measurements showed significant improvement in situation awareness measures in the intervention group (those instructed in Transcendental Meditation) over the 3-month period as compared to the control group, with p levels ranging from .033 to .047 in two of the three measurements of situation awareness (perception and projection). These findings, among other subsequent studies on TM at Norwich University, led to the incorporation of the Transcendental Meditation™ technique in the curriculum at Norwich for hundreds of students as part of their resilience development program. For firsthand accounts of benefits in decision making by students who participated in the TM studies, YouTube searches on Transcendental Meditation and Norwich University will provide added anecdotal evidence.

Improving our resilience to stress is vital for everyone in a position of decision making. Gaining knowledge of how stress impacts our judgment and the factors which improve situation awareness are a step in the right direction. Regular practice of an effective and easily learned meditation technique is equally important. Accessing our inner silence at the basis of our thinking holds the key to not only effective and successful decision making but the very soul of success.

REFERENCES

—Batorski, M. (2011). *Developing situation awareness capacity to improve judgment and decision-making under stress.* (Published doctoral dissertation). Pepperdine University. Malibu, CA.

—Endsley, M. Human Factors. *Toward a Theory of Situation Awareness in Dynamic Systems* (Vol. 37 Issue 1), pp.32-64, copyright © 1995, Figure Reprinted by Permission of SAGE Publications.
—Hill, N. (1987). *Think And Grow Rich*. (18th ed). New York, Fawcett Books.
—Sandoval, A. (2005). *The influence of organizational culture on situation awareness and decision making in a simulated peacekeeping environment* (Unpublished doctoral dissertation). Texas Technical University, Lubbock, TX.
—Travis, F., & Shear, J. (2010). Focused attention, open monitoring, and automatic self-transcending: Categories to organize meditations from Vedic, Buddhist, and Chinese traditions. *Consciousness and Cognition*, 19, 1110-1118. doi:10.1016/j.concog.2010.01.007

About Dr. Martha

Martha Batorski, EdD has been actively engaged in the field of change – both personal and business transformation – for over 30 years. First, as a management consultant affiliated with DMR Group (Montreal), Accenture LLP (Los Angeles), and Grant Thornton LLP (Washington DC), and second, as a CEO working with over 50 new venture launches – entrepreneurs across the USA building start-up companies in the financial services industry. It was this concept of making business consulting for large companies available to small businesses that earned her company the Emerging Business of the Year Award from the National Association of Women Business Owners in the first year of business. She has led 15+ successful business transformation consulting projects with global Fortune 100 companies in the USA and EU in financial services, high-tech, transportation, aerospace, energy, government, retail, and the US Navy.

A middle child in a family of nine (seven girls and two parents), Martha naturally gravitated to a career that included problem-solving, facilitation, and conflict resolution. In her formative years, she was fortunate to have been introduced to the Transcendental Meditation technique, which has served as a lifelong counterbalance to the stress of balancing consulting and academics, travel, coaching, and responding to life's curveballs. In 2003, she founded Batorski Stevens & Associates, a management consultancy specializing in business transformation, along with her husband, colleague, and business partner, Derek Stevens.

Dr. Martha Batorski is a graduate of the Graziadio School of Business at Pepperdine University in Malibu, CA (BS, MS). She completed her Doctorate in Education (EdD) in Organizational Change (Pepperdine University, 2011). All these programs were completed while working full-time (with the exception of the doctoral research and dissertation, an all-consuming event).

She is a recognized thought leader in the field of business transformation, with articles published on the impact of disruptive change on emerging organization structures (Accenture), the applied use of social media in organizations to enhance leadership and governance (Grant Thornton), and transformational change (business journals). Her doctoral research on developing situation awareness capacity to improve executive judgment and decision making under stress contributed to a multi-year change initiative at Norwich University, the oldest military university in the USA, based in Northfield, VT, where hundreds of military cadets were introduced to the Transcendental Meditation technique to develop resilience, improve scholastics, and increase overall performance. The findings of this study have been excerpted and included in *The Soul of Success Vol.3* book with Jack Canfield (creator of the *Chicken Soup for the Soul* ® series).

She is a featured speaker in healthcare, business, and education, as well as the Las Vegas Convention Speakers Bureau on the topic of leadership and change. She is a past Adjunct Professor in the MBA program at Roseman University of Health Sciences in Las Vegas, Nevada, and a member of the Transformational Leadership Council.

You can connect with Dr. Martha Batorski at:
- https://www.linkedin.com/in/marthabatorski
- martha@drmarthabatorski.com

CHAPTER 4

SELF LOVE ATTRACTS SUCCESS

BY SI LIEW, RN, MBA

I was born to entrepreneurial parents who were clueless about how to connect with me. As an infant, I would cry for hours. At the time, there was a popular parenting culture to let the child cry until it stopped. My parents were overwhelmed and sent me to live with my grandmother on the farm. I can remember as an infant being in my grandmother's arms out in nature and watching birds. This experience was critical to my spiritual journey.

Growing up, I learned how an infant's brain chemistry works when their attention and needs are not met; their brains are flooded with cortisol hormone, which causes a traumatizing signal, emphasizing to the brain that the world is dangerous. This explains why I lost contact with myself and others in my early life.

My parents took me back when I turned one year old. I was living with extended family members in the same house. I could feel the energy of their anxiety, the competition, and the fear around me. I was a nervous girl, and I constantly bit my nails.

Others were constantly comparing me to my sister. She thrived in all areas. I often felt I was not good enough. In our culture, there was an old saying, "A boy is a piece of gold, and a girl is a

47

piece of cloth." At home, my sister would receive compliments because of her achievements, while my little brother would get all the attention.

My inner conversation has always been about how I need to be lovable, better, and achieve more to gain attention. I learned to become the girl that everyone wanted me to be, so I could get approval and a sense of safety. I developed the disease of trying to please people. I learned to take responsibility for others' feelings but completely ignored my own feelings and needs. Many times in my life, I was desperate for people to pay me attention and accept me, and that need made me feel emotionally overwhelmed, anxious, and depressed.

This obsession drove many unhealthy behaviors because I thought once I graduated from university, had a good-paying job, and married a good husband, I would get all the attention and love I needed. If I looked like this or had that, I would be worthy and lovable. I was constantly fighting to fix myself by just achieving more or sacrificing more for everyone. To be an amazing woman, I thought I had to do everything and had to prove more than men and others in society. With that mindset, I eventually got exhausted.

At age 16, I got into a relationship with a man who told me he loved me. I thought I finally found the love and attention I was longing for. I became a teenage mom, and my mother was devastated. She wept as if I was dead. The news spread like wildfire across the town. I began to believe I was a very bad girl and isolated myself socially. A few years later, I left the unhealthy relationship and raised my four children with my parents' help.

I later entered the workforce with advanced degrees from post-secondary institutions. I was always taught to commit my life to excellence, a strong work ethic, and respect for authority, and I was determined to work hard to try to climb the corporate ladder to the upper echelons of the Canadian corporate world and wanted to make my parents proud.

However, I was constantly challenged on two fronts: being a single mother and an Asian woman. I constantly had to battle to balance my career, my family, and blending into the Canadian working culture. To add to these challenges, I had a poor self-image and always felt I was not sufficiently qualified for a promotion.

I later enjoyed successful leadership positions in my career, but I felt that I had a much greater destiny. But still, I felt powerless to create the things I deeply desired. I thought that maybe if I became wealthy, I would be happier. I began to invest in real estate. Eventually, I ran a multimillion-dollar real estate investment business. However, I still felt unfulfilled. I thought that maybe if I had a partner, I would be happy. I met my second spouse, and we had three children together. Now I was a caretaker of my husband and all my children. I was getting sick very often, depleted in energy, and having the expectation that they would love me if I took care of everyone.

Deep down inside me, I felt depressed, anxious, and confused despite having successes in life. I was longing for a deeper connection with my loved ones and a deep sense of needing something more in life. I worked very hard to figure my life out with my mind, but with no success. Then, I started working with my own feeling and conviction, and I started to take care of myself instead of taking care of everyone else. My spouse didn't like it, and I lost my marriage.

The familiar emotion of shame, fear, and guilt rushed into me. I was worried about what my children and others would think and say of me. I felt defeated and broken that I had again disappointed my family.

One evening, while I was in my bedroom working with piles of bills and divorce papers on my bed, my children came into my room and just lay quietly on my bed, watching me busily typing away. Just shortly after midnight, I looked around and realized they were sleeping in my bed, covered up under the weight of my problems. My tears ran down my cheek. I looked at myself in the mirror and asked how did I get to this point?

I was disappointed with the broken promise of happiness by following the path planted in my mind since I was young. I felt frustrated that I couldn't seem to make enough to live my dream and support my loved ones. The heartache and fear of not being able to find a soulmate and to experience a heart-to-heart connection as I once had with my grandmother, or the joy and fulfillment that I had hoped to experience my entire life.

At that moment, I heard a voice talking to me, "Change my life!" That day, I made the decision that I would never let myself get into this situation again and would never let my loved ones bear the weight of my problems. I promised I would master whatever skill was required to live my dream and to find a true soulmate.

I let go of my ego; I surrendered and asked for Higher Guidance. I began to pray for a mind, body, and spirit connection that could help me heal and create an inner, loving relationship with myself and help me find deeply-connected relationships.

I grabbed whatever books I could find and sought mentors. I was fascinated by the profound information. I became aware of my unconscious developmental traumas, and I began to awaken. One important lesson I learned is how to change my self-image. Self-image is the belief of who we are, and this mental picture of ourselves turns out to be a life-governing device that controls our perceptions, decisions, and actions. I began to understand the reason for having these hurtful relationship patterns in my life and how it had affected every decision I made. As a child, I saw that the world didn't appreciate me. I was not important. Thus, I decided to become a nurse as my career to make myself needed. I needed to get the validation of my existence.

My sense of self-worth has always been based on how much love I received from others and my achievements to get recognized. I saw the little girl in me, witnessed her, understood her, and loved her more.

Having not set out with a strong foundation of self-love within me made me susceptible to breaks from my outside world. Looking back on my life, I was always attracted to men to whom I gave power, but this meant no good for me. For many years, I was in abusive relationships, and I found myself lost and powerless. My identity of myself was that I was a bad person, shamed my family, and not lovable; these were the things that merited my self-love and worth. I had relied on others to offer me what I should have been giving myself.

I was attracted to people to learn lessons that I couldn't have possibly learned any other way. I kept asking in my mind, "What is the lesson that I needed here?" The awareness came to me out of the blue that I had been, when I met them, out of touch with myself.

I started to practice compassion towards myself and develop a healthy relationship within me. Men had presented a part of me that I needed to learn to love in myself. They were the reflection of my unloved part inside me.

All these years with the unconscious belief that I was not good enough as a teen mom, shamed my family and, feeling not worthy, had been controlling my life and impacted me at a deep level, including my health, my relationships, my finances, and my career.

I remembered one time when I was in a personal development seminar, and the instructor kept asking:

- What was my life purpose?
- What did I really want?
- Who did I want to be?
- Where did I want to go?

I could not answer those questions. He told me to dream and keep an open mind to all possibilities. That was the first time I give myself permission to dream.

I wrote down that I wanted to be a part of the inner circle of success and empower women to overcome barriers to discover who they could be. Then I quickly closed my notebook because I was so embarrassed to tell anyone. I started to hear my inner voice criticizing myself: Who do you think you are? What do you know? What can you give? etc.

I then started to forgive myself, let go of my past and change my messages to myself. I started to build an image of who I wanted to be. I envisioned the characteristics I wanted to have and the quality of life I wanted. This practice allowed me to take on new behaviors and recognize new opportunities. I now learned that just being myself was enough and is the only key to success in my life. My life experience was the best gift to share with the world.

During those days, I wrote positive affirmations on 3 x 5 index cards and stuck them in my bathroom so that while I was brushing my teeth I could look up and see a reminder to love myself.

I wrote notes to myself that said, "You are beautiful, worthy, deserve to be loved, and happiness is my birthright." And I put them in my purse so I could read them throughout the day. I would go to bed and read a note that said, "You only have to accept healthy and deep love." I would walk out of my house and see a note posted on the door that said, "Your purpose is to serve the world."

These affirmations were instrumental in pulling me back up, reminding me of who I truly was, and reminding me to love myself. I turned from falling face down to standing up, and ultimately to get up and running again.

Another tool I used was to find people or associates who constantly cheered me up, and who would encourage me so I could keep going. I am grateful that I have family and friends whom I can call and say, "Can you tell me all the reasons I'm good at what I do?" Sometimes I just needed to hear this.

I am grateful to have Nick, my amazing partner, who believes in the power within me, telling me all the reasons why I can do it. When my doubts start creeping in, he pulls me past my limits and reminds me of "who I AM."

Today, I have grown into a woman who demands only the best for myself, and this has become non-negotiable in the way I am being treated. I put myself first and I will strategize ways to have a fulfilling life that I deserve. When you take care of yourself and put yourself ahead of your children, your spouse, your work, and your friends, you will have an overflow of love to take care of everyone and give your gifts to the world. Success is attracted to self -love.

Many of us tend to see ourselves as very small because our self-beliefs are formed from our past experiences. These experiences shape our expectation of what is or isn't possible to have in our life. Our sense of what's possible is only a fraction of the potential of our "Be-coming." What I discovered in my transformational learning is truly about creating a new relationship with yourself by discouraging old limiting stories and changing your self-image.

There is something in us that is our least loved part. It could be a part of yourself, your life or even a decision which you made and you wish you hadn't. We need to honor the learning and the gifts of all parts of our lives. They hold the key to the answer of "something more" in our life, which sets us free to choose what we want to create.

I would like to invite you to expand your awareness to the

possibilities of what you want to become and create, and transform your deeper mindset that is outside your current conscious awareness. Let go of the past and build a healthy picture of yourself.

Good mental health begins with self-love. When we love and accept ourselves completely, we can begin to change and manifest the life we love. Happiness and a fulfilling life come from first giving yourself permission to dream.

Here is my following Ten-Step Process to Self-Love:

1. Increase your awareness of your beliefs and your patterns. Gain an understanding of your pattern – is it trying to get love, avoid pain or seek safety?
2. Notice your inner conversation with yourself. Recognise the pattern and STOP the inner critics. Ask, "Is it true?" Then let it go. We must change the way we think, speak and express love.
3. Look at the least lovable part of yourself and feel the emotions.
4. Extend your compassion, empathy, and loving kindness to yourself.
5. Practice forgiving yourself and others. Look for the gift from the lesson. Be thankful for the experience and release the past.
6. Build a mental picture of yourself as who you want to be.
7. Ask yourself, "What would I love to create?"
8. Replace your limiting stories with empowering statements about yourself.
9. Surround yourself with people who believe in you.
10. Take five actions daily to encourage Self Love.

Ask yourself: "If I really love myself, what would I do?"

About Si

Si Liew is a transformational coach, speaker, author, real estate entrepreneur and a philanthropist. She holds a Bachelor of Nursing degree and a Master of Business Administration, and is founder of her personal development company that helps people to build/design their self-image which is in harmony with their heartfelt desires. Her mission is to inspire people and provide them with transformational tools that guide them to clarify their life's purpose, push through their limiting beliefs, and manifest the life that they desire.

She has been a healthcare practitioner, entrepreneur and teacher for more than 15 years, working with patients, professionals, entrepreneurs, and students from around the world. She has blended modern science, world religions, philosophies with ancient spiritual values in teaching health and well-being restorative practices. She also helps people build their dreams, accelerate their results, and create richer and more fulfilling lives.

She had taught thousands of people to discover the truth about who they are and expand their full potential. Throughout the years of her clinical practice, she has witnessed countless clients spontaneously heal from disease and return to perfect health and well-being – simply by understanding and learning how to work with their inner energy and the mind/ body/soul connection.

As a sought-after transformational coach and professional speaker, Si also offers inspiring workshops as well as transformational in-depth coaching programs committed to helping clients achieve new heights of success, fulfillment, and spiritual living.

It is her deepest passion to help others wake up to the truth of who they are, tap into their inner power, and breakthrough to their next level of success.

Contact information:
• Website: www.SiLiew.com

CHAPTER 5

FAITH IS THE SECRET TO ACHIEVING YOUR DREAMS

BY DR. RAMESH JOLLY

Visualization. It's been the rage for years, and nearly every business book teaches some version of it. Visualization can be a powerful tool; I practice it myself. Visualization without faith behind it is about as useful as a deflated balloon. You can imagine how beautiful and colorful it will be when it is inflated, but it won't provide much enjoyment at a party unless you fill it with helium.

For visualizations and affirmations to deliver your wishes, you must have faith in something which is so powerful, strong, almighty, and unshakeable that water cannot dampen it, wind cannot blow it away, fire cannot burn it, and weapons cannot destroy it in any way.

Our minds are used to believing in things we can see, touch, and feel, such as our daily needs. Scientifically this stimulates outdreams, visualizations, emotions, and feelings. I was unable to get any emotional feeling into my affirmations without a secret tool - faith in my superpower. This faith secret changed my life and my business.

I found that having such a powerful special tool on my side was essential to focus my intentions and eliminate any doubts and fears that this superpower would manifest my dreams. After that, my affirmations, visualizations, and positive thinking worked perfectly. *This faith in my higher power was the anchor.* Without my superpower, I was able to visualize and say affirmations, but doubts lurked in my mind asking, "Who will deliver the results and manifest my dreams?"

When we make affirmations and visualize them, we should know exactly what we want and expect from these actions and affirmations. For a long time, I read my affirmations, visualized them, yet doubted them on a subconscious level. Until one day, the realization came naturally.

I am not a hard-core religious person in terms of how you pray, but I have always believed in God – or a superpower or super energy – due to my upbringing and my mom. Having been born in India, my God always has a special shape, picture, and location I can visualize or relate to. A relationship with the divine comes to people in different ways, but I visited the Vaishno Devi shrine for the first time in 2003, and many more times after I recognized in my mind that Mata Rani (the mother deity) was my superpower. Now, every morning while I am doing my prayers, no matter which country or wherever I am, I speak out my affirmations and visualize the shrine clearly in my mind and have the utmost faith that my desires will manifest with Mata Rani's blessings.

In my religion, Mata Rani is the mother deity who fulfills the wishes of her children. I feel my soul to be part of her. Superpowers, when your faith is strong, are right next to you where your body ends and your soul begins.

Faith is the anchor which enables you and your soul to move more freely by making you feel strong, daring you to act and move toward your goal without fear, and giving you the confidence that the superpower will take care of you. Your soul communicates at a subconscious level with the superpower to deliver the results. It is a beautiful process that most of us have experienced in times of great difficulty or when we are totally helpless. Faith, when combined with prayer, provides a direct link to the subconscious. In my experience, faith is the ultimate resource the soul needs. This faith needs to be pure, flawless, and unconditional. You need to totally surrender to the superpower in the actions you need to take. Take the very best actions you can take to do your part under divine guidance, then leave the rest to the superpower to deliver your dreams in its divine time.

KEEP PHYSICAL REMINDERS OF YOUR SPIRITUAL GUIDE

Regardless of whatever form of superpower-God you have faith in, keeping a physical reminder makes it easier to visualize and believe that the superpower will deliver your affirmations. I also find it helpful to keep a physical reminder of the superpower nearby or on my person to help form a stronger bond and to foster feeling loved and protected. Statues, pictures, icons, crosses, or other images that focus your attention on your relationship with your superpower will serve as reminders to rely on that power throughout your day.

SEEK POWERFUL PROFESSIONAL ASSISTANCE

Often, when we want to make a major decision or start a major project, we consult with an expert for their knowledge and wisdom. Similarly, when you want to manifest in your life, it is wise to consult your superpower resource to make the final decision. Communicate with this higher power as you would with other professionals. You will need to learn to master this communication method and faith tool. This is something that has worked for me, and I'm very happy to share this to help you achieve your dreams.

PRACTICE POSITIVE AFFIRMATIONS

You are well on your way with a manifestation of results and fulfillment of your dreams by doing things more precisely. The first step towards fulfillment of your dreams is to recite positive affirmations to clearly define your true soul's intentions, dreams, and goals. These affirmations should be so real that you feel very emotional while reading them, and later, when reciting them from your heart without needing to read them. You can do this whenever and wherever you want. Your affirmations should be a shortlist of what you desire most, and they should be in the present tense as if they have already occurred.

Your goals must be well-defined. Be specific, as you would be when ordering food in a restaurant. You need to define what you are ordering and expect to receive. I believe that my goals and dreams are now permanent ideas in my superpower's mind and must manifest themselves with nothing to prevent them.

VISUALIZE YOUR SOUL'S INTENTIONS

Another secret is the visualization of your soul's intentions, dreams, and goals as if they have already come true. This is the hardest part of this activity. You must visualize every aspect of each goal in as much detail as if you are watching a movie in which you are the star.

Affirmations and visualization go hand in hand. Sincerely repeat your affirmations a few times a day, at least in the morning when you are ready to start your day and at night before you go to sleep. Do it in a place in your home where you feel calm and can focus, so you can visualize your affirmations as you say them. Your goals and dreams need to vibrate at a higher frequency than the noise and regular vibrations of daily life. Morning and night are the best times when your mind is clear and not crowded by daily chores and activities. You will find these actions will energize you and give you a positive outlook for the day, and your subconscious mind can work on them while you sleep.

It has been said that our thoughts become things; therefore, it is crucial that our thoughts are precise, as the subconscious mind does not discriminate between things you want and things you don't want. It only knows you are thinking of those things. Think about and visualize only the things you want.

TRUST YOUR SUPERPOWER

I believe that only when the soul, heart, and brain synchronize with your affirmations do things start to happen. I believe my superpower provides essential power and support in delivering my affirmations. Whoever you choose to have faith in can be described as your guardian angel. You need that divine power always to be part of your affirmations and visualization, giving you the faith that your desires will manifest.

You must have ultimate faith, love, respect, and gratitude towards this superpower to give it the power and energy to drive your goals and dreams into reality. Have patience. All dreams and wants will manifest at the right time, not too early and not too late, in the divine's time.

I had to learn to trust my superpower. In 2007, when I was taking my company public in London, near the end of the process there were some critical things that needed to happen for us to be able to go public. We hit a roadblock that nearly prevented us from going public. There was a meeting scheduled with the regulatory broker at which a final decision was to be made. I felt helpless, unable to see what to do. I closed my eyes before the start of the meeting, and suddenly I saw a very large vision of a Durga/ Vaishno Devi statue I had at my home, but so big it stretched from earth to the sky. Within 30 minutes of that vision, we had answers and a solution that everyone agreed to. We had been unable to find a solution for 48 hours before that with many intelligent people around the table. From that point on, I trusted my anchor and superpower and felt that whatever I asked for and visualized with faith would be delivered to me.

I began to feel Mata Rani next to me everywhere. In my life, amazing things have happened out of the blue, at a fast pace, moving things and people into place without obstacles. I also started to realize that when there are too many obstacles, it is a sign that things are not meant to be.

In 2014, Sears closed in Canada; my company had over 20 stores inside Sears. I lost several million dollars of hard-earned money, but I did not give up, thanks to the grit instilled in me from my upbringing. With Mata Rani on my side, the only thing that nobody could take away from me, I had the strength to go on. My faith became even stronger.

At this time, my financial and other dreams were very visible, and one day during my prayers, a number appeared to me of my specific wealth goal. I had no exact plan for how this would be achieved but had faith that it would happen. I got a break working in a real estate land development with a hotel project for relatives buying large acres of land, improving the zoning/use, and selling it. I worked hard and sincerely on this land project, with no specific plan as to how fast the rezoning would happen or what the profit would be. The family I worked for had their own financial expectations for the property. Amazingly, the zoning approvals, rezoning, and design were quickly approved. Out of nowhere, many large real estate developers desired this land, even though there was plenty of land available in the same area, some even cheaper. We started receiving offers much higher than our goal.

Encouraged by the interest in this land, the family's financial expectations increased weekly. I prayed even harder for a successful deal. I had concerns that the potential buyers may change their minds as there was a disconnect on profit expectations. My faith, conversely, continued to become stronger and more persistent. I prayed a half dozen times a day and practiced my affirmations and visualizations. I would only receive my share of the profits when the land was sold. In the end, the profit from this deal was more than 7X the initial goal and all within a quick turnaround of 18 months. Developers who have been in this business for more than 30 years were blown away by these results.

I can see that my faith in my superpower Mata Rani brought about these amazing results and removed my hardships. I believe that a lot of this was due to my efforts and actions, but somebody else was also directing the show and delivering these exceptional results. Mata Rani delivered the results I asked for, the magical number which had appeared to me earlier. Sometimes we forget that we live, breathe, and prevail because of the superpower's discretion, or God's, and not our discretion. If you can come to grips with that, it will make you a humbler and more honest person in this life and will earn you true respect.

BE GRATEFUL

Through my faith secret, I have discovered great benefits and blessings as I continue to achieve my soul's intentions, dreams, and goals. "Jai Mata Di," I often say out of my love and affection for my superpower and thank her for her blessings always. It is this faith that is the key and most important resource. It manifests by bringing the right people, right connections, right inspired actions, and right resources at the ideal time into our lives to deliver and manifest our results. You must do your share of the work and take your responsibilities very seriously, based on your abilities. In my opinion and experience, when your superpower wants to deliver your affirmations and desires, things will happen out of the blue, and nobody will be able to stop it from manifesting. This is the comfort I have from faith.

I am so grateful every day for what my family and I have in health and wealth. If you are continually grateful for what you already have and thankful to your superpower, then other things you desire will come true and manifest into your life. The secret is that having this real superpower as your anchor will deliver the wishes conveyed by your subconscious mind.

BE HUMBLE

Sometimes we get what we want, and we lose touch with our superpower—what a waste. I have, at times, fallen off the track. This is human nature that many times when we have success, we forget how we got there and who delivered those fortunes. Fortunately, when my chips were down and there were no direct results, my superpower resurrected me again.

Negative thoughts and doubting the superpower to deliver my dreams sometimes worked against the laws of attraction in my life. We human beings have these tendencies. There are clearly many milestone blessings and achievements in my life from my childhood up to now, not because I was born in a wealthy and powerful family, but because my dad taught me that we were rich and powerful in our faith and heart.

This faith secret allowed me to have fewer fears and doubts, which are primary enemies to attaining results. Fear in your mind creates negative feelings and prevents joy and wealth from coming into your life. Through my faith in my superpower, I have no doubts about my manifestations.

Even as this chapter is published, miracles have happened for me. My biggest dreams have come true suddenly, out of the blue, in the divine's time. I am overcome by emotion and gratitude for Mata Rani's blessings for great health, success, and abundance. I am moving forward to help the poor and needy and to share her faith tool. What will you accomplish with your superpower's help, moving forward with faith?

About Dr. Ramesh

Dr. Ramesh Jolly has been a serial entrepreneur for over 35 years. With his extensive experience in taking initiatives and converting them into opportunities in the global markets, Dr. Jolly has learned through achievements and hardships the instrumental key to reaching success. Success goes well beyond being smart, able to adapt quickly, having passion, and drive. Having discovered this key facet on his own, Dr. Jolly strives to share his life-learnings with others who desire to manifest their dreams, large and small.

Recently, Dr. Jolly has been focusing on real estate development and hospitality through his venture Finial Capital and exploring projects in innovative food products and cosmetics.

Prior to Finial Capital, Dr. Jolly served as the Chairman of Pari Beauty and President and CEO of Faces Group of companies. Both companies involved cosmetics and skincare product manufacturing and retail operations of company-owned and franchisee-owned locations that operated in five different countries. Under Dr. Jolly's leadership, Faces Cosmetics went public on London's AIM Stock Exchange.

As President and CEO of Alexandria Personal Care Products, his brand gained distribution on major television shopping channels in the U.S. and Canada and was distributed throughout Canada in drug and mass merchants.

Dr. Jolly earned his Ph.D. from Cornell University in Ithaca, NY, and his B.Sc. in Dairy Technology from NDRI, India, with Gold Medal standing. He shares a U.S. Patent with Dr. F. V. Kosikowski, specializing in enzyme modification of foods and cheese. His research work at General Foods and Pfizer Pharmaceutical Research specialized in modified plant proteins, fermentation-derived proteins, enzyme modification of proteins. Dr. Jolly has another patent on Enzyme-modified proteins from Pfizer. Dr. Jolly had his own two cheese manufacturing operations growing the business tenfold and selling to majority Dairy players in Ontario, Canada.

To contribute back to his community, Dr. Jolly serves as a member of the Masonic Society in Canada and Rotary Club International. He is also involved in several Vaishno Devi projects in India and North America.

Contact:
- Email: ramesh@finialcapital.ca
- LinkedIn
- Facebook

CHAPTER 6

IT STARTS WITH YOU!

BY FERDOUS AHMED

I am Ferdous Ahmed, a restaurateur... and a successful restaurateur at that. I have been running my business successfully in Scotland for the past 22 years. It's something I am passionate about, something that I enjoy – serving great food to people and providing them with exemplary hospitality. I believe my services to be second to none. I graduated from Colchester Institute of Anglian University around 1995 in Hotel and Catering Management.

My commitment to my trade was recognized by the people, as I received numerous awards in my tenure, including the Scottish Healthy Choice Award and the Investor in People Award. I feel myself to be truly blessed, not only in terms of success in business but also in my family life. I have two great sons, Yhasin and Shafin, and my lovely wife Marilyn, who I am so proud of as a supportive and caring spouse, as she taught me how to be a better father and husband for the past 30 years, and many friends who treat my family like their own.

This is my story of how I almost gave up on life at the start of 2020, yet somehow, I still managed to turn it all around to make myself a much healthier and happier person in just seven weeks. My early days were full of struggle, being an immigrant from

Bangladesh who came to this beautiful country almost empty-handed. My journey was relentless, as I kept struggling to make things better and forced myself through hard labour day-in and day-out.

But all my hard work finally paid off as I was able to establish two restaurants while maintaining a growing family. 2019 was an especially great year for me and my business, especially for my Selkirk Restaurant. The Christmas season was extremely booming for us. So much so that I decided to further expand my business in the coming year. At the start of 2020, I invested heavily in new equipment and in strengthening our online presence on the most popular digital platforms. I had really high hopes for my future...

Then there was that news... the news saying that a new virus that originated from China was raising concerns on the global level and killing people quickly. We, however, didn't think much of it. After all, we have world-class medical facilities and the best healthcare system in the world. We have highly qualified and trained professionals who can deal with almost anything; the same was the case for Europe.

In March 2020, things took a turn for the worse when our Prime Minister Boris Johnson announced on media that the country would be going under lockdown, and businesses such as mine would be closed for an indefinite period. We weren't prepared for this... I know I wasn't...

To think that a country like ours was surrendering to a virus was the last thing we could have imagined. I couldn't think straight. My mind spun like a tumble dryer with dozens of questions popping up in my mind every second, for which I couldn't find the answer anywhere. Both my restaurants were shut down, and even though we were receiving a supporting incentive from the government, which was better than nothing, I failed to get a hold of my thoughts.

I had a few mortgages to pay. I feared what would happen if I failed to pay them… Would my house be repossessed? How would I keep up with my borrowings? What would happen to my employees who depended on my business to provide for their families? Could I show up to my friends and family with my sad face? The questions resonated in my mind… louder and louder. As the media kept breaking bad news stories one after another, it deepened my depression. My sleep was completely destroyed, so much so that one evening, the accumulation of negative thoughts in my mind became so condensed that I felt cold blood running through my body. I felt like choking on air, and I feared I was having a heart attack.

The next thing I knew, I "jumped" out of my bed like an antelope, with every passing second infusing a sense of impending doom on my nerves. I rushed to the living room and started jumping around like a headless chicken just to cool myself down. Then started the acidic build-up in my stomach that made me sprint to the toilet. This particular event would repeat itself 3 to 5 times a day for me, even at night. I wanted to scream my lungs out and cry – only to find I was unable to help myself – so I sought help externally and dialled to get a doctor's appointment. The waiting period was _ten days_ due to the pandemic.

So I turned to the internet for help, where I discovered helpful information on panic attacks. Google helped me discover a lot about this condition and even directed me to a video by an Irish Psychologist, Dr. Harry Barry, where I discovered the _Grounding Technique_. This is where you let a panic attack pass through you while staying still. You see, every time an attack ensued, I tried to run from it, tried not to think about it, and that, in turn, made the attack worse. The Grounding Technique works by convincing your mind that you aren't in any form of danger. I must say, the method worked like a charm! Then I began research on why was it happening to me in the first place, and I could point my finger in three directions:

1. First and foremost, I wasn't in the present. I was either in the future or the past, thinking about what could go wrong or regretting the mistakes that I made.
2. My diet was mostly meat, sugar, and caffeine.
3. I had no defined sleeping pattern, with most of my free time being spent on social media. This caused my mind and body to get out of synchronization due to little rest and due to my body having to work overtime with little to no energy it needed. I was always tired, even before my day began; mornings were becoming difficult for me and leaving the bed was a battle.

Presently, I'm a little better, but I still have minor episodes of panic attacks, which means I need to do better. With plenty of time on my hands during the lockdown, I started to read self-help books, a lot of them actually. This included topics like health and ageing, psychology, mindfulness, and meditation. I discovered that you could have plenty of energy for your days and a good night of sleep waiting at the day's end with the right diet. But with the wrong food and drink, you could suffer from low energy, anxiety, and depression.

So, what were my three steps to recovery? Well...

1. Living in the Present:

What does it even mean to live in the present? Well, you are already physically present in the present; you just have to be mentally here as well. My mind was often dwelling either in the future or the past, thinking of events that could happen/go wrong or regretting my mistakes from the past and pondering why they happened in the first place. Even while I was driving, my mind was 'absent,' and I drove on "mental autopilot" without paying attention to things on the route. I completely missed items like beautiful trees, children going to school, a mother pushing her child in a pram and friends greeting me on the side of the road. It was like they didn't exist for me. Friends would often complain of my ignoring them on the road, and I would turn red from embarrassment. Even the conversations at the dinner table would go over my head as I would be so lost in my thoughts. Though my mind was apparently busy with thoughts, it was racing – giving birth to problems like panic attacks, anxiety and depression.

Guilt, regret, resentment, grievances, sadness and bitterness, and all forms of non-forgiveness are caused by too much past and not enough presence.
~ Echart Tolle.

It was a problem that I needed to rectify ASAP. So I turned to meditation, which wasn't easy at first because every time I would try to meditate, my mind would sprint out of control. Eventually, I started to get a hold of it and saw actual benefits. I now have a daily routine of meditating twice a day with punctuality. It taught me a valuable lesson, which is *gratitude.* Gratitude is about being genuinely grateful, willing to acknowledge the good in life – showing appreciation for each little pleasure life sends your way. After my morning meditation, I would daily thank the Lord out loud for all the blessings He has sent my way, like my family, health, work, and anything else I can remember at the time. It changed me drastically and made me happier, calmer, and enthusiastic. For a heart that expresses gratitude is a happy heart; gratitude and remorse cannot house the same heart simultaneously.

2. A Healthy Diet:
The second step is perhaps the most difficult one, as it is really tough to maintain and requires sheer will. What you need is a balanced and simple diet; it works like a charm, actually. It's not that easy at the start, but over time, it converts into a habit. So, in the morning, I'll start with a session of meditation followed by a glass of lemon water (a medium-sized lemon squeezed in mineral water). I prefer still mineral water as it's free of any chemicals, and I keep it at room temperature. I also add in a pinch of flake sea salt for additional minerals that my body needs. Call it my daily morning ritual. This is followed by a cold shower for at

least three minutes, and when I say cold shower, I really mean *COLD SHOWER*. Then I'll have my breakfast – a cup of pure organic coffee with a spoonful of "Dave Asprey's Bulletproof Brain Octane Oil," a banana, and toast with organic grass-fed butter.

My lunch usually is a cup of rice with either fish or organic chicken. My early evening meal will be a bowl of mixed vegetables or bananas with a cup of camomile tea. In all honesty, this menu was based on a whole lot of experimentation to determine the right combination of foods that would be best for my already upset stomach. In retrospect, I eliminated processed food and sugar from my diet and replaced them with good fats which were vital for my overall wellbeing. Believe me, when I say this, it still works out to this day. We all have a different combination of probiotics in our gut, so working out the right combination of food is not an easy task, and it's definitely not a "one size fits all" matter, as we have been led to believe. There are certain foods that can lead to inflammation of the guts and severely upset your digestive system, which you need to avoid.

I do admit that in the past, I never even thought of paying attention to such minute details that could make differences of such magnitude in our daily lives. Organic was never a preference for me, but it sure is now. These days, farmers are more focused on yield and how the production looks instead of keeping it pure and original. Fruits and vegetables are now cultivated to look good, and animals are forcefully injected with antibiotics to keep them healthy.

All of this influences our overall health, our immune system, and, most importantly, our mental energy levels. With a mere change to a mindful diet and cold showers in the morning, I started to feel more energetic and became more productive. Additionally, I became more peaceful on the inside. My diet doesn't bloat my stomach anymore, and due to having a peaceful mind, I sleep really well at night – in fact, too well.

3. Peaceful Sleep:

Of all things, what had really impacted my mental health was the lack of proper and peaceful sleep. With the changes I have made in my lifestyle, I now know that in order to have a good night's sleep, I have to plan and act, eat right and do all the things throughout my day perfectly well to finally have the rest I craved. Undisputedly, a good night's rest is of essence to overall health. Eating late, and on top of that, food that didn't agree with my gut, as usual for me, was one of the primary reasons for my poor sleep. The cherry on top would be my use of a smartphone or laptop, which emits high power garbage light (aka, blue light). You see, our eyes have to work extra hard to process blue light, which in turn drains our mental energy.

As surprising as it may sound, a tired brain can't go to sleep, which is why it takes a couple of hours for our brain to regain the energy it needs to sleep. So if you spend a lot of time under fluorescent lights or on smartphones before bedtime, it can take a toll on your sleeping pattern and gravely upset it. We all know that magnificent feeling we get when we wake up from a good night's rest. Our body may rest for the entire duration of sleep, but our brain keeps working, releasing hormones to clean, repair, and rebuild our body from the inside. Yes, I can put a hand to my heart and say with all honesty that yes, you should sort out any and all issues surrounding your sleep, as it will make a massive difference in your everyday life, including your work life.

These practices can all make a difference in your life and those around you, especially your family. Meditation is not a tribal trend anymore, as an increasing number of researchers are admitting to its benefits and how it can make a difference for our health. Yes, food is, in fact, vital for our health, but that doesn't mean that one should just go with the flow. Think before you make a move, no matter how trivial it may seem. If you truly want to leave a legacy behind, not just for your family but for your community, wake up now and think about how you can better yourself. The best you can do for everyone is to better yourself, your hobbies, your habits and pave a path for others to follow in your track.

Believe in yourself. If I can do it, so can you!

About Ferdous

Ferdous has served his community with excellent quality food and service for over 21 years. He is an award-winning restaurateur and a franchisee of a fast-food chain.

He was recognized by Investor in People – UK, Scottish Healthy Choice awards, Scottish Borders Tourist Board awards, and numerous others. In addition, he has been in various newspapers and magazines for his achievement in the trade.

Recently Ferdous completed a course on Science and Health: an evidence-based approach with Open University and is now studying a course on Investigating Psychology. In addition, Ferdous worked with Jack Canfield and Patty Aubery and completed a course of Reignite Your Life with them. He also worked with Les Brown and conducted a study of Power Voice.

Ferdous enjoys supporting Young Life and serves as a member of his local Rotary Club of Selkirk with his wife, Maria. He was also served as the President of Rotary – Selkirk in 2017-18. Ferdous has two grown-up boys Yhasin and Shafin.

Contact information:
- aferdous.fa@gmail.com

CHAPTER 7

FINDING THE SOUL OF YOUR SUCCESS:
HOW MISSION-DRIVEN BRANDING PUTS YOU AHEAD OF THE PACK

BY NICK NANTON & JW DICKS

They had been best friends since they were kids – and, as adults, they had decided to go into business together. They opened one small ice cream shop that turned into a local sensation – ironically, because a sinus condition made it difficult for the one partner to taste anything. They pumped up the flavors in their frozen concoctions to such an extent that it clicked with the college crowd that frequented the area.

The store became instantly successful. On the first anniversary of its opening, the owners held a "Free Cone Day," where they gave away a free ice cream cone to every customer. That and a yearly film festival they sponsored helped make them a vital part of the community. Their local support mushroomed.

But money was still a huge problem – in the winter, there was more of it going out than coming in. They began to study brochures put out by the Small Business Administration that cost

20 cents apiece at the Post Office. They franchised a couple other stores in the region. They began selling pints of their ice cream flavors to local stores. And finally, they began to see some real money coming in.

That's when they began some soul-searching. These two guys had been almost-hippies who had grown up in the 60's, so they wanted their business to represent that spirit. They wanted to put their social mission at the center of everything they did. They wanted to always have what they called "the double dip" in place – profits and people.

They started with their own people. They put in place a policy that no employee's rate of pay would be greater than five times that of entrylevel employees. In 1995, that meant entry-level employees were paid $12 hourly and the CEO could only be paid $150,000 annually.

Then they moved on to the world at large. At the end of each month, the two of them would ask of themselves and the company, how much had they improved the quality of life in the community?

As the company's need for capital increased, they resisted venture capitalist financing, which typically requires relinquishing significant control over the company. Instead, it sold stock to residents in the region, keeping the company in local hands. In 1985, it officially created a foundation, to which the company would contribute 7.5 percent of its pretax profits.

They also made social activism a critical aspect of their operations, putting into action such projects as:

- An original scoop shop made of recycled materials
- Creation of a "Green Team" in 1989, focusing on environmental education throughout the company
- A company bus equipped with solar panels
- The use of hormone-free milk in its products

- A commitment to reducing solid and dairy waste, recycling, and water and energy conservation at the company's facilities

Ben Cohen and Jerry Greenfield's Ben & Jerry's ice cream brand ended up with annual sales of over $250 million by the end of the 90's – and was sold to Unilever for over $325 million in 2000. Today, it's regarded as the top premium ice cream brand in the world – and, even though it's now owned by a giant corporation, it still continues to deliver on its social mission to this day.

Ben & Jerry's discovered the soul of their success by always making sure their business had a soul. No doubt such iconic flavors as Cherry Garcia and Chunky Monkey helped propel them to the top – but, just as importantly, it was also the company's bigger societal mission that encouraged people to both invest in them and buy their ice cream. A 1995 article put it this way:

> "As the stockholders made clear, their investment in this ice cream company has less to do with its profitability than how it goes about making its profits. What Ben & Jerry's offers its investors is the chance to buy into a company that reminds them of themselves. A company that is innovative and impassioned about its product, but also values-driven. A company with a freewheeling sense of humor, but also a serious commitment to its community. Business on a human scale, in other words..." [1]

Or, as co-founder Jerry Greenfield himself said, revealing the real secret of their brand:

> "...we knew that's what would separate Ben & Jerry's — even more than the great flavors, it was important for us to make our social mission a central part of the company." [2]

To really discover the soul of any business's success, it's necessary to have in place a strong mission that goes beyond the usual profit

1. Carlin, Peter. "Pure Profit: For Small Companies That Stress Social Values as Much as the Bottom Line, Growing Up Hasn't Been an Easy Task. Just Ask Ben & Jerry's, Patagonia and Starbucks." *The Los Angeles* Times, February 5, 1995.
2. Harrison, J.D. "When We Were Small: Ben & Jerry's." *The Washington Post,* May 14, 2014.

motive that drives most entrepreneurs. When you're mission-driven, you have the opportunity to create a powerful and lasting brand that can continue to draw customers, grow profits and do good things for the world all at the same time.

Without that mission, however...?

Well, Unilever, the multinational conglomerate that bought the company in 2000, found out the answer to that question. After Ben and Jerry sold the business, the brand went into a slump because, first of all, the brand's true believers thought the founders had also sold out the company's mission – and second of all, that turned out to be largely true.

Unilever effectively shut the founders out of any decision-making and also curtailed the do-gooder missions of the company. To them, all that stuff was just some kind of marketing ploy.

That's why, in 2004, when Walt Freese was named as Unilever's CEO, he quickly invited Ben and Jerry back into the fold to reinvigorate the company's mission – and, of course, the brand itself. Once that mission was again completely back on track, so was the company. How important is that mission to this day?

Well, in 2010, Jostein Solheim, a Unilever executive from Norway, became the new CEO of the company and had this to say about the transition:

> "The world needs dramatic change to address the social and environmental challenges we are facing. Values-led businesses can play a critical role in driving that positive change. We need to lead by example, and prove to the world that this is the best way to run a business. Historically, this company has been and must continue to be a pioneer to continually challenge how business can be a force for good and address inequities inherent in global business." [3]

3. "Division President: Jostein Solheim, Ben & Jerry's Homemade," FoodProcess ing.com, http://www. foodprocessing.com/ceo/jostein-solheim/

In other words, in the case of Ben & Jerry's, the mission and the business were inseparable. Each made the other all the more powerful. It was the soul of their success.

MISSION-DRIVEN BRANDING: THE NEW PARADIGM

It used to be enough to make customers feel something – even if it didn't necessarily have a lot to do with your actual product or service.

It was "the Age of Emotion" for branding. In the words of Advertising Age:

> "Prompted by booms of products and prosperity, conspicuous consumption kicked into high gear, and logic wasn't enough. Your product had to make a prospective buyer feel something. A car was freedom on four wheels, jeans made you rebellious."[4]

Yes, branding used to be all about tugging the heartstrings. For example, back in the 1970's, the classic heartwarming Coke commercial featuring football player "Mean" Joe Greene throwing a kid his jersey would make a nation sigh and open another bottle of Coke. McDonalds' famous song-and-dance "You Deserve a Break Today" campaign would motivate families to give Mom the night off from cooking and go get some Big Macs, while Kodak would sell its cameras and film with sentimental family photos and a goofy Paul Anka jingle, "For the Times of Your Life."

Today? Because you can instantly take photos with your phone, Kodak is virtually out of business. The Coca-Cola Company is under fire for allegedly causing obesity and is desperate to repair the image of its signature product. And McDonalds? In 2013, when it began soliciting positive customer comments on Twitter,

---

4. Walker, Abbie. "Brands Need to Know Their Purpose and What They Aspire to Be," *Advertising Age*, February 24, 2014.

it instead got overwhelmed with tweeted horror stories from the public, leading the campaign to be dubbed "McFail."

Technology and the Internet have changed everything. That, in turn, means manufactured emotions delivered by an ad or a commercial will only get an organization so far these days. As the same Advertising Age article goes on to say, "Our brands ask consumers for what a person expects from his or her friends—loyalty, trust, attention, love, time—without putting in the reciprocally requisite work. In other words, brands need to reconsider their motivations and behaviors because no one is buying the be-our-friend act any longer."[5]

In other words, trying to manufacture an emotion without having anything real behind it just won't do the job for a business anymore.

That's why Mission-Driven Branding is a must for this day and age. When an organization genuinely takes on a mission and implements it inside and out, when it is consistent and authentic in pursuing that mission, that organization has a far greater chance of creating loyalty and trust – and of creating an authentic emotional response – than by constantly reinventing its appeal with gimmicky short-term marketing campaigns.

There are two huge factors in play today that are an enormous threat to any company trying to win over customers and clients with superficial marketing tactics:

1. There's too much information out there.

Abraham Lincoln famously said, "You can fool all the people some of the time, and some of the people all the time, but you cannot fool all the people all the time." That's never been more true than right this minute.

For example, a few years back, the Chick-fil-A restaurant chain

---

5. Ibid

was embroiled in a firestorm over its backing of anti-gay policies. At the time, a sweet-looking teenage girl rushed to the company's defense by writing earnest posts on her Facebook page detailing all of Chick-fil-A's wonderful qualities. But, because the Internet is the Internet, somebody quickly figured out that this girl's picture was licensed from a stock photo company – and the media presumed that Chick-Fil-A had most likely set up the fake account to manufacture support for its positions, even with no real evidence to prove it.[6]

In other words, whereas a brand might have been able to get away with these kinds of practices before, there is virtually no chance of it now. Even if Chick-fil-A hadn't put up the fake Facebook account, the Internet "jury" still found the company guilty by association. And this was far from an isolated case – right now, there are now millions of amateur "branding police" actively investigating which companies are trying to pull a fast one and which ones are being authentic.

The Mission-Driven company has a natural advantage in this punitive climate. When it stays true to its mission, an organization can't help but pass the "smell test" on the Internet and elsewhere. It earns respect rather than derision from its actions – and that respect boosts its brand above the competition.

2. There are too many choices out there.

With all the options out there for a consumer, and all things being equal, how is that person going to choose who to buy from? Or perhaps the bigger question is: Why would that person choose to buy from a certain company or individual over another? Being Mission-Driven gives your company the answer to a customer's "Why." By defining how your brand uniquely serves the customer or society at large, you also define the positive role of your brand in that person's life.

---

6. Johnson, Dave. "Did Chick-fil-A's PR use fake Facebook account?" CBSNews. com, July 30, 2012. http://www.cbsnews.com/news/did-chick-fil-as-pr-use-fake-facebook-account/

Let's go back to a few of the brands we already talked about and see how their missions add value not only to the brands themselves, but also to a consumer's buying experience:

- If you want yummy ice cream and you want to make the world a better place, you buy from Ben & Jerry's.
- If you want a good chicken lunch or dinner and want to support a company that shares your values, you buy from Chick-fil-A.
- If you want a smartphone and want to buy from the company with the most innovative and stylish technology, you buy from Apple.

In each of the above cases, the company's mission gives the consumer a strong, concrete reason to buy from them – and to continue buying from them. There will always be plenty of premium ice cream brands, chicken restaurants and smartphone manufacturers to choose from – but Ben & Jerry's, Chick-fil-A and Apple all bring a whole lot more than their actual products to the consumer marketplace. No, their individual missions don't resonate with everyone – but they resonate strongly enough with a large enough base to keep their brands incredibly profitable and continually growing.

Again, being Mission-Driven is not really an option in today's marketplace – it's a necessity. As FastCoExist.com put it, "Today's brand must live and breathe through its core values in order to survive. Purpose is king, and there's no turning back."[7] And, in the words of Charles Schwab's executive vice president and CMO, Becky Saeger, "to be successful today, you must identify your company's purpose and execute like crazy."[8]

---

7. Blotter, Jennifer. "10 Ways Today's Purpose-Driven Brands Can Bring Their Core Values to Life," Fast- CoExist.com, October 14, 2013. http://www. fastcoexist.com /3019856/10-ways-todays-purpose-drivenbrands- can-bring-their-core-values-to-life
8. Adamson, Allen. "Define Your Brand's Purpose, Not Just Its Promise." *Forbes*, November 11, 2009.

MISSION-DRIVEN BRANDING:
HOW IT DELIVERS THE FIVE BIG "D'S"

We'd like to close this chapter by naming what we've identified as the "5 Big D's" – the 5 biggest benefits that a successful mission can bring to any brand:

• DESIRABILITY
The right mission attracts a fervent and loyal customer/client base all on its own. When that mission is organically attached to the brand in question, the brand not only attracts buyers, it also attracts quality employees who want to be a part of the brand's mission. Apple again is the best example of this principle in action, but there's no question the quality of Desirability applies to many, many other Mission-Driven brands as well, such as Disney, Patagonia, or Zappos.

• DISTANCE
Any brand faces the danger of losing its luster over time. Remember when Atari was the only gaming choice in American households? Or when you could find a Blockbuster video store in every strip mall in the neighborhood? In contrast, having a firm mission in place – and, just as importantly, continuing to make that mission relevant (imagine if Blockbuster had been the first to do what Netflix did) – almost guarantees consumer loyalty and an ongoing high profile in the marketplace, allowing a brand to truly go the distance.

• DEPENDABILITY
A mission helps a brand retain a consistent identity in the public's mind over the long haul. That consistency is important to developing trust and likeability with clients/customers and keeping them coming back for more. Walmart's "Save Money. Live Better." mission, for example, drives a constant stream of bargain-driven consumers through its doors, because those consumers know the retailer has a high degree of dependability.

• DIRECTION

A mission empowers a brand to focus on what it does best and provide a strong direction for the company as a whole. For instance, companies like Google and Apple understand they have a mandate to continue to deliver innovative technology that improves people's lives. That mandate, in turns, drives how they do business over the long haul and forces them to concentrate on the direction that defines them in terms of public perception.

• DIFFERENTIATION

Finally, Mission-Driven branding creates a powerful differentiation in the marketplace in contrast to the competition. Ben & Jerry's had that differentiation when they first began as a homegrown socially aware business – and they quickly lost it when the brand became just another acquisition by a multinational corporation, Unilever. For those few years, they were just another ice cream brand – and it was easy for their formerly fervent fans to simply pick another ice cream if it was cheaper or more convenient. A mission makes a company more than just another merchant or service provider – it transforms it into something much more meaningful and substantial, a business that truly stands out from the pack.

Of course, we've cherry-picked a lot of successful brands in this chapter to demonstrate the power of Mission-Driven branding. You the reader might rightly ask, "Well, yes, a mission works for big players like Apple and Google, but what real difference does it make to most companies?"

Well, we're glad you asked (even if we were the ones doing the asking for you) – because, it turns out, there is actually a concrete way to demonstrate the overall and overwhelming advantage of Mission-Driven branding.

In 2011, Havas Media Labs, one of the leading global communications and marketing groups, began compiling what they called the "Meaningful Brands Index." For the first time, a detailed analysis of companies that were Mission Driven in one way or another (through CSR (Corporate Social Responsibility) policies, sustainability, community giving, cause marketing, etc.) was done to determine just how this kind of brand activity affected their actual business.

The result? In the 2013 survey, the so-called Meaningful Brands outperformed the stock market by an incredible 120%.[9]

Umair Haque, director of Havas Media Labs, had this to say as an explanation of the amazing success of Mission-Driven brands: "People aren't irrational in what they expect. They don't want perfect lives—but they do want better lives. What we consistently find is that institutions don't meet their expectations in real human terms. When they do find companies that are willing to benefit them, they're really happy doing business with them."[10]

And that to us is definitely the Soul of Success!

---

9. Dill, Kathryn. "Google, Samsung, Microsoft Head A Tech-Dominated List of The Most 'Meaningful' Brands," *Forbes*, June 14, 2013.
10. Ibid

About Nick

From the slums of Port-au-Prince, Haiti with special forces raiding a sex trafficking ring and freeing children; to the Virgin Galactic Space Port in Mojave with Sir Richard Branson, Nick is passionate about telling stories that connect.

He has directed more than 60 documentaries and a sold-out Broadway Show (garnering 43 Emmy nominations in multiple regional and national competitions, and 22 wins). He has made films and shows featuring: Larry King, Jack Nicklaus, Tony Robbins, Sir Richard Branson, Dean Kamen, Lisa Nichols, Peter Diamandis and many more. He is currently the host of *In Case You Didn't Know...with Nick Nanton* on Amazon Prime, and regularly hosts the podcast *Now to Next with Nick Nanton* which can be found on all popular podcast platforms.

Nick also enjoys serving as an Elder at Orangewood Church, supporting Young Life, Entrepreneurs International and rooting for the Florida Gators with his wife Kristina and their three children, Brock, Bowen and Addison.

Learn more at:
- www.NickNanton.com
- www.CelebrityBrandingAgency.com
- www.DNAmedia.com

About JW

JW Dicks, Esq., is the CEO of DN Agency, an Inc. 5000 Multimedia Company that represents over 3,000 clients in 63 countries.

He is a *Wall Street Journal* Best-Selling Author® who has authored or co-authored over 47 books, a 7-time Emmy® Award-winning Executive Producer and a Broadway Show Producer.

JW is an Ansari XPRIZE Innovation Board member, Chairman of the Board of the National Retirement Council™, Chairman of the Board of the National Academy of Best-Selling Authors®, Board Member of the National Association of Experts, Writers and Speakers®, and a Board Member of the International Academy of Film Makers®.

He has been quoted on business and financial topics in national media such as *USA Today, The Wall Street Journal, Newsweek, Forbes, CNBC.com,* and *Fortune Magazine Small Business.*

JW has co-authored books with legends like Jack Canfield, Brian Tracy, Tom Hopkins, Dr. Nido Qubein, Steve Forbes, Richard Branson, Michael Gerber, Dr. Ivan Misner, and Dan Kennedy.

JW has appeared and interviewed on business television shows airing on ABC, NBC, CBS, and FOX affiliates around the country and co-produces and syndicates a line of franchised business television shows such as *Success Today, Wall Street Today, Hollywood Live,* and *Profiles of Success.*

JW and his wife of 47 years, Linda, have two daughters, and four granddaughters. He is a sixth-generation Floridian and splits his time between his home in Orlando and his beach house on Florida's west coast.

CHAPTER 8

NOT BUSINESS AS USUAL: WHAT IS SUSTAINABILITY ANYWAY? … AND WHY SHOULD YOU CARE?

BY NADA SHEPHERD, MBA

They say nothing happens overnight, but I would argue that is an oversimplification.

Erosion is defined as the gradual destruction of something, and in this story, that something was my tolerance of excessive waste in the fashion industry. As I sat down to begin this story, I reflected upon the poignant souvenir I took home after a trip to London in 2007; a gripping disappointment at the gluttonous levels of inventory that crowded each store. While years in the fashion industry gradually exposed me to the "less sexy" elements of clothing manufacturing and sales, this trip was the catalyst to ultimately shove me from the hamster wheel and force me to begin deciding what actions, however small, would bring me closer to more sustainable business practices.

With over a decade working in the fashion industry and having received a diploma in Fashion Design, I was more than just interested in the intricacies of this industry; I was mesmerized by them. As cliché as it may be, *too much of a good thing isn't always good*. The eras of the fashion industry continued to change in one common direction. Fast fashion, while positively intentioned, continued to accelerate the manufacturing process, driving excessive production and inventory that could never be exhausted before the next drop was available. My desire to contribute to this endless cycle slowly diminished, "Does the world really need another skirt?"

As someone who grew up in a household and age in which the climate crisis was "not real," I never considered myself much of an environmentalist. Especially, having worked in the fashion industry, which according to a 2018 sustainability report from Quantis, "accounts for an estimated 8.1%" of carbon dioxide equivalent emissions. The more I learned, the more I realized, business as usual was no longer a viable model for sustainable growth.

SO, WHAT IS SUSTAINABILITY ANYWAY?

My best friend also finds herself connected to the industry, working as a celebrity stylist. Both of us had begun having conversations after that fateful London trip. Excessive waste in the industry was becoming an issue that could no longer be ignored. Those conversations have continued, and often, it circles back to how sustainability materializes in the world in which we live and work. She once pondered about policies in her workplace and their relationship to sustainability: "Is that why my rental vehicle is always electric? Perhaps that's why they won't reimburse me for a bottle of water? I need to bring my own bottle and fill it up." Sustainability is more than just a greenwashed attempt to promote "environmentally friendly" practices. Sustainability is an intentional and purposeful commitment to the preservation of resources and capital – spanning human, social, economic, and environmental sources. These have become known by many as the four pillars of sustainability. Others will claim that sustainability is better represented by three pillars, but I believe the inclusion of human capital preservation cannot be ignored when seeking to embrace the sustainability principle. This belief is why I have committed to replenishing communities impacted by reduced manufacturing with financial contributions and learning resources.

But why should you care? The short answer is that your customers care. Your stakeholders also care, and if appropriate, your shareholders care. Culture and generations are changing, and an emphasis on sustainable investing and purchasing is growing in popularity. New products, new companies, new competitors are born every day, which means consumers have more choices than ever. They want to feel good when they spend their hard-earned money, and we're finding that sustainability is actually quite green, and we don't mean just environmentally.

At the time of this writing, the world is still in the grips of a global pandemic, brought on by the virus called Covid-19 (and its numerous variants). The steps taken in a noble attempt to prevent the virus from completely running rampant gave way to several catastrophic consequences. However, that is not our focus here. The global response exposed, and in many cases magnified, our world's human, social, economic, and environmental weaknesses and inequalities. Sustainability has been offered the spotlight at center stage.

You might be doubting the weight of your impact. Thinking to yourself, "I'm just a small business owner. Sustainability policies are meant for multi-national corporations." My goal is that you will walk away with a renewed confidence that whether you are a small business owner, mid-management professional, or C-Level executive, you can embrace sustainability practices – and you should!

Let's start by digging deeper into the four pillars of sustainability:

1. Human Sustainability

"A great employee is like a four-leaf clover, hard to find and lucky to have." I may not have written this quote, but I understand how true it is. Human sustainability is focused on preserving and contributing to the betterment of human resources in, and related to, your ventures. This takes form through staff development initiatives, preventative health care, food security, and other measures to protect human capital. The reach that a business should consider goes beyond those that directly contribute to your operations, but also includes those that are impacted by proxy of your operations.

2. Social Sustainability

The ripple effect occurs when an initial action or event causes a progressively larger reaction and result. Simple cause and effect is a concept that we learn early in adolescence. Yet acknowledging and accepting how our actions can impact others is a more complex lesson to learn. Social sustainability can be seen as the next step from human sustainability. Considering more than just the basic needs to maintain human capital, but a commitment to moral and inclusive business practices. Again, it should be noted that this commitment is extended both to those engaged within the business and those impacted by the business, like the communities in which the business operates. It is the commitment to refuse exploitation and magnify empowerment.

3. Economic Sustainability

Unless you are a not-for-profit organization, maintaining profits will always be a priority as a business owner. The question becomes, "At what cost?" Economic sustainability means overhead is sufficient to monitor expenses and manage resources, such that profits are maintained. The challenge, however, is balancing economic sustainability against the damages incurred in the process. If human and social sustainability positions a business to safeguard human capital and promote empowerment and inclusivity, economic sustainability should build upon this foundation to embrace measures that responsibly consume resources while maintaining profitability.

4. Environmental Sustainability

What many may improperly reduce sustainability to represent appears as the fourth pillar. Environmental sustainability pursues the advancement of human well-being while preserving natural resources like land, water, air, etc. This pillar encourages businesses to implement controls that support achieving their strategic goals while minimizing the impact of their operations on the environment.

It can feel overwhelming to embrace the principle of sustainability without the resources of a multi-national corporation, but it doesn't have to be. One simple activity you can take on today: reflect on the industry you belong to, and with an honest, unbiased eye, identify the ways your industry conversely impacts one of the four above-mentioned sustainability pillars.

Patagonia is an extraordinary example of a member of the clothing manufacturing industry that started their sustainability journey long before many businesses adopted mindful practices. They are not unlike other giants in the industry, whose revenue is directly dependent on selling clothing. This common activity is one that has many negative environmental, human, and at times, social and economic impacts.

However, Patagonia made the decision early to develop clothing that lasted longer, reducing the need for excessive manufacturing.

Today, in 2021, Patagonia is currently a certified B-Corp with an impact score of just over 151, a 41% positive increase since starting in 2011. Becoming a certified B-Corp is one of the many ways a business can qualify its commitment to sustainability. Businesses are awarded points based on the following areas:

1) Governance
2) Workers
3) Community
4) Environment
5) Product Services

It is a process rooted in evolution, and the keyword here is process. A business may choose to focus solely on its workers and environmental impacts or may focus on incorporating measures in all areas. Even an environmentally-conscious company like Patagonia spent a decade increasing their B-Corp score, corresponding to a more fulsome approach to sustainability practices and governance. Achieving holistic sustainability does not happen overnight. Through many small but deliberate actions, you can promote sustainability within your business, and by extension, your industry.

A formal B-Corp certification is just one of the many certifications available for organizations looking to embrace sustainability. Others include, but are not limited to Fair Trade, Energy Star, and LEED. The point to be made is the boundless opportunities for both businesses and professionals alike to lean into more mindful practices; ...and don't worry, you'll be in good company.

Sustainability has become mainstream and the "feel-good trend" of our time. This is confirmed as more than 90% of S&P 500 companies now produce an annual sustainability report, compared to only 20% in 2011. Not only is sustainability the new movement, but in many cases, it is also the expected norm. Remember when we said sustainability is actually quite green; would you believe me if I told you the S&P 500 Environmental & Socially Responsible Index has outperformed the S&P 500 consistently. Just check the numbers. Customers and investors are interested in metrics other than financial returns. It is no longer sufficient to solely prioritize shareholder profits.

Incorporating environmental, social, and governance (ESG) practices can be the first step towards more sustainable operations. At my soon-to-launch startup ReSuit, I've baked ESG right into the DNA. As a small-business owner, I own my responsibility to contribute to the shift required of an industry whose negative impacts outweigh its positive. My commitment developed as a dedicated percentage allocation of every transaction into our "Do Good" budget, earmarked for re-education initiatives in communities most impacted by a reduction in clothing manufacturing.

Now what? There may be hurdles for you to overcome as you seek sustainability. Maybe you're bound by bureaucratic red tape within a large organization, or maybe it's hard to imagine how a small business can commit to sustainability while still turning a profit. I've included five easy-to-start tasks no matter where you fall on the spectrum.

1. **Look Inward:** As a business owner or leader, your work becomes a reflection of your values and principles. Reflect internally to understand what is most important to you and make a note of that. Use these notes to align your sustainability strategy to your passion. Doing something you love will nevertheless make the work worthwhile.
2. **Look Outward:** That simple task we said you can take on today, starts with an unfiltered assessment of the industry to which you belong. Where can improvements be made? What are the expected challenges or hurdles you may have to overcome in your goal to achieve more sustainable practices? When you feel like you don't know what question to ask next, just ask, "Why?" Keep asking until there is no further explanation, and then you will have found the root of the problem you seek to solve.
3. **Create a Vision:** With methodical reflection complete, you

are armed with the appropriate context and motivation to begin shaping your strategy. You must know yourself, know your business, and know your industry. Then, it's time to develop your North Star. A well-defined vision guides strategy development and fuels your flame when the going gets tough.

4. **Start Small:** Develop specific, measurable, and attainable goals to gain early wins in your efforts towards sustainability. Remember, it's a journey, not a destination. Slow and steady will build momentum, encouraging you to stay the course and remain committed.

5. **Get Support:** Whether you are securing an executive sponsor or networking with other business owners, support will keep you afloat. Allow others to inspire you, challenge your perspectives, and offer insight and wisdom. While a sponsor has the power to bolster your efforts in a broader organization, as a business owner, the power resides in your influence to bring others on your journey.

So, what does *sustainability* mean to you?

About Nada

Creating a more sustainable world starts with big ideas. Nada Shepherd gives life to those big ideas, crafting actions that are tangible and impactful.

First, the bona fides: Nada is an Ivey Scholar with Distinction, possessing an Executive MBA from the Ivey Business School at Western University. She holds a B.Sc. in Neuroscience and Psychology from the University of Toronto and a Diploma in Fashion Design, a unique combination of expertise that has propelled her to success in a variety of industries.

Nada spent a decade in the fashion industry as the Founder and Creative Director of two labels, NADA and nadanuff. Her designs were seen in major North American publications, such as *Elle, O Magazine, InStyle,* and *Redbook.* Named one of the Top 3 Designers to Watch by Jeanne Beker at Fashion Television in 2007, Nada had a first-hand look at how the fashion industry works: the good, the bad, and the ugly. Nada was engaged at every intersection of the business, including managing an entire supply chain with both domestic and international components.

It was through this experience that Nada was exposed to the amount of waste created by the fashion industry, but as she evolved, the industry around her began to slowly shift. However, there was, and is, still a long way to go.

In an industry that exalted consumption above all else, what does it mean to be sustainable anyway?

Enter ReSuit, a business venture that Nada founded in 2019 and is set to officially launch in 2022. When her daughter was born in 2014, Nada began developing the ReSuit business model to combat excessive production and greenwashing of the modern fashion industry. ReSuit is built to have no inventory; it is a fit-based, peer-to-peer clothing rental and resale app with a mandate of sustainability.

Some will argue that nothing in this world is free, and when it comes to sustainability, Nada knows this to be true. There is a cost paid by those who have lost their jobs – mostly women – due to the movement to reduce clothing consumption and embrace slow fashion. Nada seeks to understand the whole story, not just the headline. That is why ReSuit aims to make a measurable difference in the lives of those affected by clothing manufacturing job reduction. Through financial contributions and resources, the communities impacted the most are not left to foot the bill of sustainability.

In addition to her work at ReSuit, Nada also owns and operates a boutique consulting firm, White Space Shepherds Inc., that provides creative and technology-driven solutions for clients throughout the North American market. Co-founded with her husband, the firm helps to shepherd businesses through the unknown. Particularly, they have focused on assisting tech startups in establishing a firm foothold in their industries.

Nada lives in Toronto with her husband, two young children, and her cats and dog.

To learn more about Nada's work, make sure to follow her on Instagram, and visit:
- www.resuit.com
- www.whitespaceshepherds.com

CHAPTER 9

'LIVING IN GRATITUDE' A MANUAL FOR DAILY PRACTICE

BY GOPI NAIR

Live in gratitude and remain grateful day and night, regardless of what challenges one has to face. This is unconditional gratitude. Conditional gratitude expects certain benefits to be received to be grateful. When a person remains grateful under all circumstances, he is unconditionally grateful.

"Do you mean to say that I should be grateful even when 'bad things' happen. For example, my father just passed away. Are you asking me to be grateful for this painful experience?"

Yes!

Your father just finished his mission and departed. Understand that his death is not the end of his life. It is the end of a life cycle – one cycle ends, and another begins. Rest assured yourself! This is an appropriate time for you to express your gratitude to your dear departed father, especially for all that you have learned and inherited (spiritually) from him. Secondly, your mind is rattling like a rattle snake, rattling restlessly as the image of your deceased father temporarily deranges your mind. An ounce of gratitude introduces immediate sanity to your mind. Gratitude, realistically speaking, is the ultimate 'mind cleanser.' It removes all the negativities in their entirety. A mind devoid of negativity is fresh and creative, ready to take on any tasks. Third, with the onset of new freshness, you can do a better job of consoling your mother and your siblings to help them regain their composure and peace of mind. After all, life is all about taking care of others. You can be that 'anchor' your family just lost.

Start the day with gratitude. As soon as you open your eyes in the morning, before getting out of your bed, say a prayer of gratitude. If you are religiously oriented, read a prayer of gratitude from your scripture – whether it's the Bible, Gita, Quran, Talmud, or any other scripture.

Just before you retire for the night, while in bed, recite the following affirmation:

"OH! ALMIGHTY GOD! I AM GRATEFUL FOR THE ABUNDANCE OF HEALTH, WEALTH, HAPPINESS, AND KNOWLEDGE."

Gratitude is not only a good attitude, gratitude must be the only attitude in life. When you show gratitude at all times to everything and everybody, they too change because you change. Every circumstance you encounter is your own creation. When you think about the 'hurt' more and more, it sinks deeper into your subconscious mind.

The secret of training the mind lies in understanding the harmony between the Master mind {conscious mind) and the Servant mind {subconscious mind). The master is the discriminating faculty of man. It is the thinking mind, the reasoning mind. It works on the basis of inductive reasoning. It compares the facts and arrives at logical conclusions. It is the rational mind. Our logical thinking is the very nature of the Master Mind. It thinks logically, like

A=B, B=C, therefore A=C. By definition, being the obedient servant that it is, the subconscious simply obeys the command of the Master Mind.

The subconscious mind, by definition, works on the following basis:

1. It works on deductive reasoning.
2. It is amenable to suggestion.
3. It transcends Time and Space.
4. It is an inlet into the universal mind, where every thought ever produced by any man is stored and kept.
5. The paranormal qualities, like clairvoyance, psychokinesis, telepathy, etc., are the normal faculties of the servant mind.
6. It is the source of all power.
7. It believes anything that is impressed on it. It is like a sponge.
8. It is the builder of the body and the source of all healing, both physical and emotional.

You need to understand gratitude as a mind cleanser. It is the elixir for removing negativity. Gratitude must be the only attitude in life. Count your blessings and write them down.

Gratitude simply neutralizes your mind. It takes you to the Higher power – God or whatever name you choose to call this Higher Power – for every solution. A mind devoid of negativity is 'Divine,' peace alone dwells there. And a 'Divinely absorbed mind' is a creative mind, as it can attract anything from anywhere to find a solution to your problem, however challenging it may appear to be at the outset.

This is the healing power of gratitude. It simply restores harmony instead of discord. It is not what happens to you that matters, but how you perceive it or process the information. Gratitude is an invitation to Divine intervention, not dictating what should happen but surrendering to the Higher Power to be in charge of the situation. You refrain from wishing ill to anyone, but deliberately 'wish well' to all parties involved. You wish for others what you wish for yourself (Jainism). The same is echoed in the Bible as the Golden rule, that you treat people the way you wish to be treated. A grateful mind is the abode of abundance. It can attract wealth, health, harmony, happiness. It is the why or when of the salvation or freedom from bondage. The key is training your mind to be grateful; always remind yourself of that.

What is Negativity, and how does it affect our daily lives?

The best way to define negativity is to know it as darkness! Wherever there is no harmony, there is negativity. The Law of Harmony is the Supreme Law of the Spirit. The very unity of spirit, that state of tranquility, is harmony. Where there is harmony, there is peace and plenty; where there is no harmony, there is negativity. Negativity can be compared to darkness. Darkness is the condition caused by the absence of light. Similarly, the moment harmony is introduced, negativity is erased.

Negativity has multiple faces. Vanity, anger, fear, hate, depression, and even despair are all made of negativity. Negativity is the mother of all ailments – bodily, mentally, and emotionally. It is the raw material with which all negative emotions are created. It drains our positive energy and makes us vulnerable and exposed to all kinds of diseases. If the immune system breaks down due to the constant exposure to negative energy, the same poison that inflicts the body also inflicts the human mind.

What are common negative energy exposures?

1. *Gossip:* We are sipping the negativity that arises during a gossip exercise, and worse, we do not even know about it.
2. *Hate:* This is a very dangerous exposure to negative energy. It unleashes negativity into our systems, and it profusely drains our positivity.
3. *Fear:* Fear is a very common and yet little understood negative emotion. It has very different stages, starting with simple fear – if left unchecked, it can lead to panic and anxiety attacks.

Remedy – Love what you hate and do not allow fear to take root in your mind.

MIND/BODY CONNECTION

We all know that mind and body are connected. Now modern medical science, after many years of research, has announced that there is something called Mind. It can cause disease and ailments. The very term 'psychosomatic' means – 'psyche' affecting 'soma' – the mind affecting the body.

Every emotion is the manifestation of the Mind-Body connection. Positive emotions like Love, Compassion, Mercy, Forgiveness, and Care all positively impact the soma, while negative emotions like Fear, Jealousy, Hate, Vanity, Anger, etc., affect the 'soma' negatively.

The Supreme Law of Spirit is harmony. Once you learn to dwell on the plane of harmony, you remain healed at all times. Healing means a feeling of oneness where there is no conflict, no stress. You are literally living in the present, and you are at peace with yourself and the Universe.

So remember, gratitude is the eternal light that erases the darkness of negativity. It can be compared to the Sun, which is the ultimate dispeller of darkness in the Universe. Just like light and darkness cannot coexist side by side, gratitude and negativity cannot coexist.

Therefore, a heart filled with gratitude cannot entertain any kind of negativity. It simply is impossible. Remain grateful at all times and remain in the present. Gratitude is the facilitator that helps you enjoy the present, whatever it may be for you.

About Gopi

Gopi Nair has been a Gratitude Practitioner. He embarked on a mission to change lives for the better by encouraging everyone to practice Gratitude. Gopi is convinced that Gratitude is a magic wand capable of removing negativity from the shores of the human mind! If one is devoid of negativity and its energy-draining consequences, they can realize their full potential. "Gratitude must be the only attitude in life" is Gopi's mantra. *He thinks Gratitude, speaks Gratitude, and relentlessly does Deeds of Gratitude in everyday life.* We all can give the gift of Gratitude to others to enrich their lives along with ours!

Gopi has been in sales for over four decades, and that gave him an opportunity to interact with thousands of people. He used his insight into emotional wisdom to navigate through the world of sales successfully. While he was working with MetLife, he qualified three times for the prestigious Presidents Conference and several times for the Million Dollar Round Table. During his career with MetLife, he trained several Agents in his capacity as a Manager.

During the last twenty years, Gopi Nair has been a Mortgage Broker and currently works with Guaranteed Rate as a Vice President, Mortgage Lending. Gopi has been a published author, having published *Mental Science 101, Manage Your Mind Manage your Life, How I made 500,000 in Sales at Age 69,* and *Tablets of Emotional Wisdom.* His new book, *Gopi's Gratitude Journal,* was published recently. Gopi's philosophy of life can be summarized as follows: "When you live for yourself, life is utterly miserable. When you live for others, it is pure joy!"

Gopi had the privilege of being interviewed by Jack Canfield, the famous author and Creator of the *Chicken Soup for the Soul®* Series, about his book *Tablets of Emotional Wisdom.*

Gopi Nair graduated from the University of Bombay with a Master's degree in business. He migrated to the States almost half a century ago. He is an Inspirational Speaker, always willing and available to speak about the Power of Gratitude in changing lives.

You can connect with Gopi at:
- Tel: 630-290-6847
- Email: gopi132@yahoo.com

CHAPTER 10

"CAN WE AUTOCORRECT HUMANITY?"
~ Prince Ea
CAN WE BUILD A WORLD OF HOPE?

BY JULIE MEATES

Miraculous Messages Motivating Masses from Matariki Stars

A tribute to all those affected by natural disasters and war, and to all those we love, especially our mothers. Thank you for your inspiration. Marvellous Meghan, Clever Charlotte, Joyful Jack, Joe, and many others. Those shining stars and wonder filled leaders making a difference to save the world. Have faith. The future is bright. Dreams can come true.

Awaken in morning light, a new dawn has begun; sun silhouettes through trees, exhaustion released. Interlinked reflections following many minds' contemplative paths, seeking wisdom to share a message of hope-divine intervention. Journey into the Miracle Zone (Marci Shimoff – Year of Miracles) – one of the last vestiges of forest, an intergenerational legacy – Christchurch, New Zealand.

Faces from around the world seek this happy place, where nature has been preserved for centuries. The market found in nature is filled with folk of all races, creeds, ages, and nationalities. All are happily chatting – cell-phone-free – in the fresh air with blue skies surrounding them and a faint mist blown in from the river's flowing crystal clear current.

Media can have remarkable effects on our lives and has repeatedly captured history as it is happening. It reflects the key themes and tone of a society at any moment in time, serving as a time capsule for future generations. In 2021, Sir David Attenborough narrated the Apple TV documentary *The Year Earth Changed*, in which he remarked, "…if we choose, we can transform the health of the planet, for all."

As humanity, we have been given an opportunity to pause and reflect with greater focus. To deny avoidance and embrace active consciousness. The Covid 19 pandemic was a magnifying glass, exposing weaknesses in our world, like a stone in our shoe, an uncomfortable reminder of the fragility of our earth, our common home and the weaknesses caused by humans' modern day life. Although you may have felt locked down, remember the power you hold, with grace and the rich mosaic of faith. The soul of success is promoting a better world for future generations. It is a commitment to health, wealth, and happiness, but, not in the traditional understanding of these principles, fostering these as tenets for our global community. We believe that no one person, group, community, civilization, or otherwise should achieve these at the expense of another. Success is not an accident on the road of life. It is a mindful decision. Communities that care make a better place.

For you are an ace. Light your soul on fire. Did you know there are superpowers lying dormant within you, waiting for you to unlock them? Within your consciousness and thoughts, below the surface of your mind, telling you there's more to life. A higher calling...

For life is for living and forgiving. Don't sweat the small stuff.

Start the day with love in your heart
~ Og Mandino.

Meandering through Riccarton Bush Market, Kathryn Glen's radiant, loving, joy-filled smile beamed. Her shiny hair glistened as she spoke confidently, her voice pure and clear, like the crystal-clear river that flowed so near. Know your purpose and your goals. As Stella said, stick with it, be resilient. Be true to your values. All rowed in waters protected by ancestry and were under 23.

HEALTH – like a favorite jacket or vest that protects you. Look after your body: it houses the temple of your soul. Feed it loving thoughts and healthy foods and water for like the turtle dove, when in harmony it can bring peace – maybe world peace, for no dream is too big. We've been ravaging our internal rainforest, as much as we've been ravaging the ones outdoors, with devastating effects. Trust your gut.

Help and heal and hear and humor. Treat others as you would like others to treat you – the secret ingredient is laughter. Here laughter fills the air. Listen. Robert Consedine's message, as an author to the world, is clear: Heal our history and heal ourselves. Show compassion to others and to yourself.

Sir Mason Durie is an emeritus professor from New Zealand who developed *Te Whare Tapa Whā,* a model defining four dimensions of wellbeing.

- physical wellbeing
- mental wellbeing
- spiritual wellbeing
- family wellbeing

When visually represented it appears as a house with four walls represented by each dimension. The abundance or lack of care we offer our physical wellbeing will surely affect our mental wellbeing. It is harmony through all dimensions that we should seek. Family extends beyond those that share our blood, including the human family.

Our connection with the whenua/land forms the foundation. Without one of them, it is like driving a car with only two wheels. Neglect one at your peril, for so often we neglect some and wonder why we may feel empty, in an existential vacuum that only God can fill. For like a car, when all these things are in balance, we thrive and can drive. Let love not fear, be your fuel.

> *Outer pollution is a sign of inner pollution.*
> ~ Eckhart Tolle.

The pollution of the planet is only an outward reflection of an inner psychic pollution: millions of unconscious individuals not taking responsibility for their inner space.

If humans clear inner pollution, then they will also cease to create outer pollution.

[The above quotes from *THE POWER OF NOW: A Guide to Spiritual Enlightenment.* - (2010), p.78-79, New World Library by Eckhart Tolle.]

So, clean up our messes and turn those messes into messages for the greatest gift to humanity in a sick world is to heal yourself. The greatest act of kindness is to be aware of your unconscious thoughts, then softly help others to heal too, for heal is the first four letters of the word health. Think KIM – Kind, Inspirational, Magical.

Awaken with a positive and enlightening attitude and fill your days with authentic and courageous conversations. Awareness brings knowing – a knowing like the opening of the Pike River open cast mine; where death and darkness pervades, or like a heart afraid of breaking that never learns to...love, as Bette Midler put it. There is a shifting consciousness, an opening of the divine if we but look. Know your creator – Yazu. What if we innercized and exercised as John Assaraf suggests? Could the consciousness of the planet shift?

As Lisa Nichols says, peel back the layers of self in order to grow. Expose the lies and find the truth. Are you lying on a nail or taking an action to improve things? Reveal the dormant wellspring of love that resides inside.

Welcome! Do you know how amazing you are?

While life can be disappointing, frustrating, maddening, and sometimes hard and blunt, life can also be incredibly innovative, integrated, resilient, and outcome-focused – we have no other choice. Open-mindedness and belief in a great life system operating and universal principles of love, kindness, respect, and peace are key. No matter what happens we can orientate ourselves to face the light or the shadows, and feel flat, or turn the axis so the music in our soul plays a beautiful melody. It is that simple. For like life, we can lie flat on our back or bounce back like a basketball. The latter gives you a better shot at life and success. For even in a pandemic, life is not what happens to you but how you deal with it.

$$E \ (event) + R \ (response) = O \ (outcome)$$
~ Jack Canfield.

Like a deck of cards, you sometimes hold the ace card or the joker. Laughter is a key and it is one of the things in life that is free, like the sunrise and sunset we get to start each moment fresh, and each dawn starts a new day. Remember that. Have no regrets. Mistakes are only missed takes.

As Mark Twain said: "The two most important days in your life are the day you are born and the day you find out why."

*   *   *

WEALTH? – For life is like a kaleidoscope. Sometimes it is dark but sometimes darkness transforms the natural world into a different world for darkness turns into light, just as the night becomes day but if you turn it a little, you get a different perspective.

"In a world that is changing really quickly, the only strategy that is guaranteed to fail is not taking risks." Mark Zuckerberg

(*Juno* magazine, 2021, p. 46). But what if some risks have dire consequences?

As Lisa Nichols says in *Abundance Now*: *"If Wealth is so much more than money, how do you know when your nest egg is enough?"* (p. 231).

"The cell phone rings. We are connected. We are implicated. We're all in it." (Womankind, Lema Shamamba, p.131). Unfettered, the war had gripped at their country, with massive repercussion: more than five million lives lost, rainforests decimated. The peace of the past that languished in the land was now marred by bullets, rape, and memories that left undeniable pain and trauma in the people of this area of the vastly inhabited country. As the documentary alludes: *Is the Blood in the Mobile* soullessness or success?

Like other courageous women in the DRC who had stood up to injustices and were hope in action, Mama Jeanne Nacatche Banyere and Mama Jeanette Kahindo Bindu remind us through their message to the world: *'Crisis in Congo: Uncovering the Truth.'* We have to understand what is going on. We don't have another planet we can hide on. As the rainforest is decimated in her homeland for the coltan for our cell phones and computers, and lithium for our batteries, Lema reminds us we are all connected. Big companies still harm Mother Earth. We throw things in the ocean and our water gets polluted. This is not the soul of success.

> *Turning a blind eye to this tragedy is being complicit.*
> ~ Dr Denis Mukwege, Nobel Peace Prize Laureate
> from his work at Panzi Hospital and City of Joy.

That mysterious black box that can wreck havoc on your soul, as Blessed Anna Maria prophesied.

Pope Francis asks what planet have we created through exploitation and degradation? What sort of ancestor bequeaths this perilous situation to their children?

*   *   *

As Susan Krumdieck discusses in her book *Transition Engineering*, allocation and management of our common resources is an ancient and time-held practice essential to sustainability. Villages exist around the world where families have farmed the land and lived in the same houses for 600 years. Management of these common resources ensured that resources were not overtaxed for future generation's wellbeing. These principles have ensured a soul of success for thousands of years, but as Susan says, traditional systems have been broken down by new technologies that allow faster extraction. This is at the cost of the planet that we must treasure, for there is no planet B. Do we want a world filled with plastic, soulless to be fantastic?

A Journey of Hope that raises awareness, a well world, a rallying call to action to protect our rainforests, and the abolishment of modern-day slavery of mining of coltan and supply chains, sustaining People and Planet – that is the ultimate soul of success. As Walt Disney said: "If you dream it you can do it." Leave a legacy that changes the face of humanity and save our earth.

For the true measure of any society can be found in
how it treats its most vulnerable.
~ Gandhi

We are all in it together, interconnected – beacons of hope. Like a woven cloak, the strands can unravel or we can weave beautiful embroidery. Make it the masterpiece it was created.

Plant more trees. Plant more hope. Even better, protect the existing rainforests, the Amazon and especially the Congo – the world's second-largest rainforest. **The world's largest forest carbon sink**, with its ability to store greenhouse gases, creates a healthy ecosystem that buffers the spread of the pandemic and mitigates climate change. Make it a planetary vision – a healthy planet. We depend on it for food, clean water, and clean air. Yet, the trajectory seems intent on destroying it so fast because of business interests. Take care of it.

But there is hope. What if the best was yet to come?

Take 100% responsibility.
~ Jack Canfield.

Jane Goodall's Trillion Trees Project is a Soul of Success. Jack Canfield's *Success Principles* is a Soul of Success, and with Mark Victor Hanson, their vision for reforesting the planet with 18 billion trees is a Soul of Success, as is preservation of pre-existing rainforest. That is how about many we deplete each year. Make a Garden of Eden.

Sir David Attenborough in *A Life on Our Planet - My Witness Statement and Vision for the Future* lays out actions to save the planet – "Prioritize people and planet over profit alone." (p. 134). Protect the forests. "We have one final chance to create the perfect home and restore the wonderful world we inherited. All we need is the will to do so." Great leaders like Joe collaborate.

Remember *The Soul of Money – Transforming your Money and Life* by Lyn Twist, and karmic investments.

You only have one life to live. Supercharge it by harnessing your mind's true power and unlocking the secret to more – the biggest calling – *Te reo o Te Ao*, the voice of the world.

Sometimes it falls upon a generation to be great,
you can be that generation.
~ Nelson Mandela.

HAPPINESS – Like Bach's story of Jonathon Livingston Seagull, our big audacious dream of world peace may seem insurmountable but have hope and purpose. For you are never given the dream without the power to make it happen.

Invest in happiness. Instead of carrying a chip on your shoulder, carry an angel of joy. She holds our hands and touches our soul. Let me look at your eyes for they are the window to the soul. They are beautiful. I love you. Look at others as if they have

Jesus within them. Show compassion, a true friend to every one of us; the gift of seeing the best in us and made us feel valued and special.

Here is a summary of *The Four Agreements* by Don Miguel Ruiz:

1. **Be Impeccable with Your Word** – As we previously saw in the dimensions of wellbeing, mental wellbeing is fed with loving and caring thoughts about yourself. Tuning the inner voice to speak truths encourages the denial of self-criticisms that do not support your growth and success. This extends to those around us, reinforcing the importance of family wellbeing. Maya Angelou is famously quoted saying, *"I've learned that people will forget what you said, people will forget what you did, but people will never forget how you made them feel."*

2. **Don't Take Anything Personally** – Empathy further deepens our connection to others. It may feel most natural to assume that someone's actions towards you have something to do with you. However, this agreement encourages you to consider that their actions have nothing to do with you and more to do with that person's sufferings. This releases you from being the victim and empowers you with clarity and compassion.

3. **Don't Make Assumptions** – Making assumptions can lead to many avoidable conflicts. Clear communication allows both parties the opportunity to define their needs, expectations, thoughts, or feelings. This agreement silences the internal voice of judgement by eliminating the ammunition of a poorly calculated assumption.

4. **Always Do Your Best** – It wouldn't be fair to complete the list of *The Four Agreements* without a quote from Ruiz himself, "If you have done your best and the Judge tries to judge you according to your Book of Law,[1] you've got the answer: 'I did my best.'" Peace comes when regardless of an outcome; you can say that you gave 100%. Your best may change from situation to situation, but it is your commitment to do your best to enjoy the process.

1. *If you judge people, you have no time to love them.* ~ Mother Teresa

Some days, maintaining these agreements with you will be easy. Other days, it may be a challenge, and we won't get it right every day. Make sure to give yourself empathy and start fresh the next day; do your best.

When the three principles of health, wealth, and happiness are in harmony and prioritized for all, we all reap the benefits. We find the *Soul of Success.*

We are called now to prioritize the health of our bodies, minds, spirits, and relationships. We must expand our quest for wealth to include plains of rich experience and valleys of valuable lessons. The life we must seek is one abundantly filled with love and wisdom, continuing to evolve as we lean further into our purpose. Acknowledge the clockmaker and relinquish to a higher power, and through this release, harness the power of your freedom and achieve true happiness.

Bill Gates reminds us: "At the end of each year, I still enjoy taking stock of my work and personal life." (*Juno* magazine, 2021, p. 47).

As new challenges emerge, take time to reflect on Four Rs of Deep Adaptation by Professor Jem Bendell:

1. **Resilience** – what do we value that we most want to keep?
2. **Relinquish** – what could we let go of that doesn't make matters worse?
3. **Restoration** – what can we bring back in these challenging times?
4. **Reconciliation** - with whom do you want to make peace while we can, as we awaken?

What that message may sound like tomorrow is the subject of prayers, thoughts and actions today. Choose every day to preserve this world for each of us and for the generations yet to come. Little steps can make big changes. Start today because we're already a day late. It now rests in your hands. Let's be on the right side of history. What's stopping you?

About Julie

Julie Meates is a New Zealand-born humanitarian endeavouring to bring more peace, kindness, and love into our world. Her career has been multifaceted and varied. For her, family has been important. She is married with three wonderful children and a wide, diverse, extended family.

Julie has a passion for education and health, starting her early career as a teacher. She has also qualified as a social worker, counselor and is now a barrister and solicitor, and is currently involved in post-graduate work in education and health. She is passionate about community wellbeing and has worked in a volunteer capacity in many roles – with the mantra and hope that kindness will be paid forward.

In 2002, she was the co-founder of the Fulfil A Dream Foundation with a vision of strong and happy families, strong and vibrant communities, and wise and visionary leadership – empowering individuals, families, and communities. Fulfil A Dream Foundation was fortunate to work with high-profile musicians, sportsmen, politicians, community, education, and health leaders. Julie was also the chairperson of a Maori learning centre (indigenous Kohanga reo).

Currently, Julie is a volunteer with community law's programme of community justice panels. The Community Panel process aims to repair the harm caused by the offender promptly, using restorative justice processes. She has been a volunteer on the United Nations executive in her Canterbury region as Board Secretary, and presently with the inception of Women of Hope Wake Up and Help Ourselves Trust Board.

She has been involved over the years with Women's Refuge and several other NGO/charitable institute non-governmental organisations – COGS (Community Organisation Grants Scheme). She was vice president of the International Community Organisation (Wairarapa International Communities Incorporated) Society and was involved in community radio doing local, national, and international broadcasts. She has also worked with the homeless nationally and internationally.

Julie has been part of many community lead initiatives to strengthen communities in sometimes complex situations, weaving together storytelling and music, and empowering youth and community talent.

She has represented sport and has coached at high school, as well as being a physical education and health teacher and tutor, and she has further qualifications in design. In her high school, she was awarded best all-round person.

Julie Meates is a quiet leader, able to inspire, influence, coordinate and empower people to achieve desired goals. Julie is experienced in working in partnership with organisations, with local communities and individuals, to make a difference. She is empathetic, positive, non-judgmental, and kind, with an ability to relate to a wide range of people.

CHAPTER 11

CAMOUFLAGE TO KHAKIS

BY MAJ. ANDREW WHITE (RET.)

I had the honor and privilege for over 20 years to serve with some of the greatest men and women in this country and perhaps the world has to offer. I learned things about myself and, more importantly, about others. What made these men and women so special, and how did these lessons inspire me to be better and want to be better. What makes a Veteran? What is our Why? It was not because they took an oath of service but because they believed in some things greater than themselves. They learned the meaning of teamwork, personal sacrifice, and pushing themselves to achieve both physical and mental challenges that they did not know they could do. I know these things to be true, because I was that soldier who learned things about myself I never knew. I learned that in the military, no matter what branch or what your job was, others depended on me, and I depended on them. These lessons I learned throughout my military service have helped guide me to success well beyond my days in uniform.

What makes Veterans so effective and why? ... TEAMWORK!

It's not just being part of a team but contributing to the overall success and achieving a command goal. As a Military Officer, I would tell my soldiers that, "No one works for me, but you all work with me, each of us has a role to play in this unit, and we do our jobs to the best of our abilities." My job was to lead. While that may seem easy enough on the surface, leading takes a lot of trust, not just for those who are following you, but for you to put faith in those around you to do their best and put them in a position that allows them to exceed those expectations. We all have strengths and weaknesses. As a leader, it was important to know what they were for each of my soldiers, and that included me.

Developing my soldiers into leaders and followers was an important skill I had to develop. I learned that in the military, there are two types of leaders, those who had the ability to persuade others to charge a hill or take a beachhead knowing that danger awaited them on the other side, and then there are those who lead by technical knowledge and experience. Both skills are important to develop in all of those subordinates. Leading troops into combat is a combination of mental toughness and personal courage. When asking someone to put their life in your hands just as you put your life in theirs, you can't hesitate or waiver. Fear is natural, but your ability to control your fear and the fear of those around you is not something that can be necessarily trained or taught to others, but rather something that is developed inside you. Only time can tell if you have that kind of courage. I would constantly tell my men to be accountable for everything they did.

I had three rules for my troops every time we left the compound.

- Rule #1: War is not like the movies and there is no director yelling 'cut' if things go wrong.
- Rule #2: There is no glory or fun in having to shoot someone.
- Rule #3: There is nothing glorious in someone out there trying to shoot you.

Those were my rules to help keep my troops (and myself) safe and controlled whenever we traveled outside of the compound. Technical leaders: These are guys who sometimes possessed the same character traits as troop leaders, but they lead by example by doing their job or using their skill set to perfection. I would always rely on these folks because I know that there are things that need a subject matter expert. Technical experts can save you so much time and headaches that can really affect your success or failure. Learning from them also gives them an opportunity to grow as leaders and build that teamwork.

I was a big believer in treating all my soldiers like they were rock stars and letting them know I appreciated them. I wanted my men to always know how much I valued them. I hated to hear soldiers tell me when I asked them what they did, "I am just a ---." (By the way, that is one of my personal pet peeves.) I never wanted anyone to ever tell me they were ... "just a ---". You are more than a 'just a ---'; you are part of a Team, and if you don't do your part in that team, well then, that team does not meet its mission or goal. Soldiers, like employees of a company, need to feel their value and know they are special and able to contribute to a cause.

When I was in the military, I would often seek out opportunities to spend time with my troops. I felt being a hands-on leader rather than an administrative leader allowed me to connect with my soldiers and form a bond that would be critical when I asked them to be placed in harm's way. These attributes really paid off, not just in combat but years later. Recently, I reunited with several of my soldiers from my first deployment back in 2005 to Iraq. It was 16 years since I had seen most of them but reconnecting with them reminded me of how WE got each other home safe from the war. That is due to the special bond and relationship we had and knowing how to rely on one another.

LEADERSHIP

The Recalibrated Carnivore:

One thing that most veterans are is trainable and our unique ability to come up with terms to describe what we do in some very colorful terms. Recalibrated carnivore is a term I heard many years ago, and when I first heard it, I was not sure what it meant, but after being around some of the troops, you learn terms and expressions that you will not hear in the civilian world. So, what does it mean to be a recalibrated carnivore? Well, when you are going through basic training, you are all taught how to be basic warriors (e.g., a Rifleman). We are all taught how to shoot, move, and communicate. That is the root of what all warriors are, but once we leave the military, we need to find a new way of doing things and how to shed that rough exterior of being a warrior and become a member of the civilian world. We need to learn how to take the drive and soft skills that the military taught us and transfer that to being and becoming something else.

Motivation:

Motivation, well this is something that can easily be blurred in both civilian life and in the military. Like I stated when talking about leadership, when the time comes to go into harm's way, you need to find that something special to motivate yourself to give that order and to motivate those around you. Everyone has their "WHY," and knowing how to motivate those WHYs is key to success in both the military and in Corporate America. Knowing what makes a person 'tick' and what they can be and do is important if you want to get the most out of those around you, and also how to create a desirable culture in your work environment. No two soldiers, like no two co-workers, have the same WHY. The best leaders need to know how to motivate everyone's WHY and make them believe in a single cause or purpose. That is how teamwork is built, and success is created. It is much easier to get those around you to believe in some things and work towards a command goal rather than force them into something they are reluctant to do.

Diversity:

This is by far the greatest life lesson I learned in the military. It was not the diversity of race or religion that I learned, but social and geographical differences. I have been all over the world and visited nearly every state in the union. I have never been in a more diversified group or place than when I was in the Military. I went for basic training in June of 1994 to Fort Knox, KY. There were soldiers with me from New York, Mississippi, California, Michigan, Iowa, and several other states.

The stories and lives that each of us had were very different. How we were raised, and our individual personal experiences were so fascinating to me. I remember thinking to myself: Who would have known that even in our own country, we could be so different? I heard stories of guys being raised on family farms or ranches and from guys that lived in the inner cities and saw the military as a way to escape gangs. I grew up in a small suburb in New England, and these things were just not part of my youth, but I was fascinated to learn about them, and more importantly, about the soldiers themselves.

The Army gave me opportunity to see other countries as well as to learn about their cultures. This really opened my eyes to the bigger picture of things. Life is full of challenges no matter where you are from or how you grow up; you can choose to stay put and never leave, but you also never grow. When I retired from the Military, I wanted my children to get a sense of what other people outside of where they were from lived and their points of view. I encouraged each of my children to go off to college far away from home, so that they too could experience similar types of exposure I had meeting new people.

Equality:

As in diversity, we all may have had differences in how we were raised, but I am a big believer that we can achieve our own desired success if we put in the effort. In the military, I had soldiers from all walks of life and opportunities. When you are going through basic training, the army breaks you down psychologically and then builds you back up. You may have been a 5-star athlete in school, but if you outrun your unit, you find yourself alone on the battlefield, much like in life. You need to learn to work with each other and realize that you are all in it together. You need to realize that in the Army we are all GREEN.

Strength development vs. weakness improvement:

You have to find ways to develop one's strength vs. weakness improvement; not everyone can do 100 pushups or run a mile in under four minutes. But then again, not everyone can hit a moving target at 300 meters or breakdown codes either. These strengths and attributes of individuals are important to building a successful team. The army would often take the super athlete, the all-American guy who everyone thought was the natural leader and make them the follower for the shy and quiet one. This was done to teach one how to follow and be a stronger leader, but it was also done to build the confidence of those who needed to find their Inner WHY. You needed to know that if one man fell, someone else would have to take his place – "Next Man Up!" That is what makes Teamwork, and a successful team rises to the top.

Adapt to change:

No one knows the meaning of change better than a military Veteran. In many cases, that is the one thing that is constant in military life. We need to change direction or adapt to new environments constantly. That is one thing we learned – stagnation and complacency are never good. We rotate out of units, move our families around the world, and are asked to do something you never expect to do. Whether it is going to war or performing a humanitarian mission, no two missions are the same. They each have their own level of difficulty and challenge to overcome. No one knows how to overcome difficulties and challenges like soldiers. That is what being a soldier is – rising up to the challenge and defeating it.

Network:

Nothing is more valuable than the ability to network. I learned this from one of my Supply Sergeants in the army. He taught me that with the right networks and connections to the right people, anything is possible. No truer words have ever been spoken. I learned to be a master in networking with people and getting things done. With everyone I talked to, I would always find a way to connect with them on some level. This proved to be most valuable to me in Iraq. I was able to make friends with folks that had contact with our food supply trucks. We provided them some security and a great place to stay whenever they would go on a convoy, and in return, my soldiers and I received lots of extra rations of steak and other hard-to-get meals. At some point, we stopped going to the base dining hall and started making meals in our little compound on the base camp. When I said adapt to change, soldiers can make anything better if you give them the opportunity.

In closing, we soldiers are a unique breed of individual. We are motivated, opportunists, and mostly dedicated to success. We will surprise you with our ingenuity in fixing and solving problems, but at the same time, we will rarely take credit for it either. That is mainly due to our sense of Teamwork, which is most noteworthy about soldiers, because nothing we did in the military was an individual action.

Even when we are recognized by awards or dedications, they are still a team effort. The best example of this is on every award. No matter what the award, it all reads the same with this last line, "… this award brings great credit upon the soldier, the unit and the branch of service they belong to." It is written that way to show that the awardee is the carrier of the award, but that award was and always is a team effort.

About Maj. Andrew

Andrew E. White is a retired US Army Major who gave over 20 years of service to his country and a never-ending devotion to the men and women of the military and their families. He grew up in Fairfield, CT, and attended Roger Williams University in Bristol, RI. In 1994, he joined the US Army and shipped off to Ft. Knox for training. In 1999, Andrew received his commission as a 2LT in the US Army, and that is where his career really took off.

Following the events of 9/11, Andrew was called up to serve as one of the first on the ground at DFW Airport to secure our nation's airport. He served as a platoon leader and was promoted to Executive Officer of the DFW, ensuring the safety and safe travel of all those traveling.

In 2004, Andrew was called up again to head overseas in support of the War on Terror by deploying to Iraq and later to the Sinai Desert.

After 20 years as an officer, Andrew White (Maj. Ret.) retired from the US Army on 02 Jan 2019. While serving in the Army, he had the greatest honor of leading some of the greatest men and women in the world. It was a privilege for him to live out his dream as a soldier. From the age of five, when he dressed up as a soldier for Halloween, he knew that was what he wanted to be, and he got to follow his dream.

Now retired and living in North Texas, he continues to serve his country by working for the government as a recruiter for government agencies and enjoying time spent with his family and friends. Andrew stays very active with Veteran groups and is always ready to help others in any way he can.

CHAPTER 12

"AM I HAVING A STROKE?"
THE 7 MOST IMPORTANT TOOLS FOR BOUNCING BACK FROM ANY TRAUMATIC EXPERIENCE.

BY KDB WHEELER

"I wonder if I am having a stroke."

It's surreal to realize that eight simple words define the life-changing event when a blood vessel bursts in your brain. Welcome to the beginning of your new normal.

Time slows as you watch your own body falling to the floor. This out-of-body experience is punctuated when your brain registers, "I'm wedged between my furniture." The left side of your body hits the ground first, and the remaining auto responses you possess send a command to your right hand, "Grab your mobile phone." Trying to grasp the phone from this angle looks like a scene from the medical drama series Transplant. Your attempt to use the phone only confirms the worst; yes, you are having a stroke.

The gravity of your circumstances weighs heavier on you with each moment. Fire Department Emergency Medical Technicians are breaking through the door. Everyone is speaking forcefully, nearly shouting as you are hoisted up off the floor onto a stretcher. The ambulance is rushing you to the hospital, with requisite sirens blaring. The emergency room professionals scramble to administer TPA medication to help restore blood flow to your brain in hopes of preventing severe stroke damage. Even through semi-consciousness, you hear everything as if you're a bystander in the next room. Did we get here fast enough? Will the medication work? Among the terrifying thoughts racing through my mind was, "And if this doesn't work, what will?"

It doesn't matter the size of the blood vessel that bursts—where or on which side of your brain it happened—your life will be impacted; routines will be disrupted. Comprehension, speech, mobility, strength, and dexterity all become distant goals in the long process of relearning, and, just for clarification, I was one of the lucky ones.

I was lucky enough to arrive at the emergency room within the critical three-hour window for the administration of the TPA medication to be effective...lucky enough to be recovering at home within three months. And I was lucky enough to be here to share my story and the seven tools that helped me achieve my recovery goals.

These seven tools are just a few of the tools I have mastered over my years. And these seven, in particular, are what became the foundation and pillars of my successful recovery. They also kept me from spiraling down into despair and reminded me of my life's purpose.

It started when I had regained enough consciousness in the hospital's Intensive Care Unit. *Affirmations* and expressing daily *Gratitude* helped me view my new reality with a more positive outlook. When the initial horror of being paralyzed on my left side felt like too much to digest, I was relieved and very grateful to learn that the paralysis was expected to be temporary—as in, it might take a year to resolve versus being permanent. I expressed my primary affirmation mantra, "I am so happy and grateful now that I have full use of the left side of my body" on a daily basis. Other affirmations were added as the weeks and months progressed.

Thankfully, the part of my brain where my comedic slant on life is stored was fully intact! I relied on humor to fuel hope in my recovery and anchor my sanity. *Monty Python's Flying Circus* captured it perfectly in one of their most remembered skits, "NObody expects the Spanish Inquisition!" This seemed more than apropos of my situation. Trust me, a blood vessel bursting in my brain was not on my list of expected plans for 2021—not even a footnote.

My plans were now being determined by the hospital's rehabilitation unit's Stroke Recovery Strategies, and my first goal was set – to leave Acute Rehabilitation walking. That goal was quickly superseded when the doctors informed me that use of my left side would only return through intense therapies—therapy in multiple forms, in multiple stages, and over time. My focus on leaving this unit walking in heels was far-fetched. As I remember this formidable goal, all I can say is, "Seriously, heels?!"

My imagination of Inpatient Rehabilitation and home recovery was an illusion of leisure and idealism. Here is what I thought I would find in an average day's schedule: sleeping in, undemanding breakfasts, and some therapy here and there; a welcomed light lunch, a timely nap, maybe a little more therapy. Why not add a proper cocktail hour, culminating in a replenishing dinner? I imagined days accented with the occasional scintillating medical conversation with technicians, nurses, and doctors. What utopian hospital scene did I float in from?

The reality of my new normal was more than an average challenge. Recovery went from a snail's to a turtle's pace. My recovery made me feel as if I were in a time warp. The process of regaining use of my left side required creativity and determination. For example, relearning how to use certain body parts was a very slow progression toward successful achievement, and the left arm and hand were not prepared to start that learning process quite yet. Imagine a fish that you toss onto the shore that is desperately trying to make it back to the river. There was a lot of flailing! With that fish in mind, I started to think of the next goal I would eventually add to the list – cooking. I could not begin to imagine cooking in my current physical state. My left arm and hand were forgetting ever having known one another. Suddenly my recovery goals seemed to compound and feel insurmountable.

Reframing gave me the power to flip my script and rewrite a new story that would move me more closely to the reality I wanted – one where I was using my left hand, arm, leg, and foot. Incremental goals would be critical to keep my recovery momentum going, as well as support my psychological and emotional well-being. All my daily activities, such as shopping, cooking, cleaning, and more, would require learning new strategies; but first, we had to get the left arm and hand to wake up. The medical staff assured me that one way this could ultimately be achieved would be through deep muscle stimulation – an incremental, achievable goal. This was a start. The next small goal involved reinforcing where the arm was located and its function at this location. Another incremental, achievable goal. Was it easy? No—Attainable? Yes. Reframing allowed me to adjust my perspective on the long road to recovery and focus on the small stair-step goals. Reframing also provided a tool to flip the negative medical information into more positive mental and emotional frameworks for me – rather than becoming any part of the negative statistics, which was not okay with me.

It was self-compassion and self-forgiveness that staved off feelings of inadequacy. In fairness, this was the first time I had ever experienced my body not responding to brain signals for movement. *Compassion* and *Forgiveness* allowed me to recognize that I am only human, and as such, I am not invincible. I allowed myself to be self-compassionate by becoming my own best friend and being kind. It even helped to recognize these moments as opportunities to view this situation through a lens of grace. I turned to self-forgiveness any time my mind wandered into the deep, dark woods where I placed blame on myself for even having a stroke. Being able to release these types of feelings helped me to promote a better sense of well-being. I forgave myself and, in doing so, allowed my body, mind, and spirit to begin to heal.

It was an example from an Occupational Therapist that really invoked my empathy and self-compassion. She explained that the area of the brain that sends signals to your arm is like an expressway. The stroke created the need for infrastructure repairs. During these repairs, traffic (aka neurological signals) was being detoured. Eventually, the expressway would be repaired and reopened, allowing the brain to send signals to my arm again. Recovery was within reach, and yet there were still challenges ahead for me to overcome.

With this new frame of reference, my focus never wavered from daily goals using other tools that were familiar and reliable such as meditation and centering.

Meditation was how I chose to start and end each day. It was also the response I chose when feeling anxious, terrified, or apprehensive. Meditation was not a new practice for me. As I've said, these tools are ones that were commonplace in my life. I had already realized many of the benefits that could be achieved by incorporating meditation into my daily habits. An expanded awareness is just one of the benefits to be expected from the accumulative effects of daily meditation and one that I welcomed during my process of relearning. Expanded awareness is said to have been practiced by Samurai, and I was taking on more and more warrior qualities—fierce determination was the first one.

Centering quieted the mental chatter, dialed down emotional fears, and created a state of internal calm. While straightforward, centering requires practice, of which rehabilitation offered plenty. Trust me though, there is no need to race into rehabilitation to start practicing! Home and work locations are more than sufficient, rather preferred, and both will produce success. Take it from me: it was because of the practice I already used at both home and work that made it easy for me to apply these principles when it mattered most.

This quickly became my "go-to" tool when relearning to walk. The breathing part of it was especially helpful. One of the many frustrating—and downright exasperating—exercises I did daily was figuring out how to get my left foot to remember it was connected to my leg. Even my left knee and hip were "disconnected". The worst of the disconnected neurological wiring was the part of my brain that kept me balanced. Watching myself in one of the Physical Therapy full-length mirrors always looked like Weeble Wobble children's toys. This was so much easier when I learned it the first go-round!

The medical staff nicknamed me the "Therapy Warrior." They cheered me on with my laser-focused determination. While they laughed at my humor, it was the music du jour, the one constant and simple tool in my toolbox, that found its purpose throughout every day of my Inpatient Rehabilitation recovery. It was the Music that the medical staff anticipated with joy. It's hard to imagine what we did before mobile phones! Now playing: *"My Life with a Soundtrack." – A smile appears across your face as you are wrapped in benevolent beats. Your brain feels focused, yet calm. A sense of peace washes over you as a blend of harmonies fill the space around you.* It is no secret that music is an effective form of therapy. Why wouldn't I take advantage of an already established habit to further my chance of success in recovery? Music was a natural, yet essential tool during this time.

It cannot be expressed enough that I was one of the incredibly lucky ones. My gratitude is overflowing today as I reflect on the amazing care I received throughout this time. I made it my mission to exhibit this attitude of gratitude with everyone I encountered. From the housekeeping staff to dining services, from the daily medical technicians to weekly phlebotomists, and everyone in between, I am forever grateful. Well, maybe not quite as grateful when the phlebotomist missed my vein and had to retake my blood. But I never stopped appreciating the overall amazing medical care. Of equal value is the support that I continue to receive from my family and friends.

It is because of these amazing individuals that I discovered a life purpose much greater than myself.

My recovery path has been paved by these life-affirming processes and practices that I now call *The 7 Most Important Tools for Bouncing Back from Any Traumatic Experience.*

Here is a recap of all seven tools, along with a brief description of each.

1. **Affirmations & Gratitude:** Gratitude comes from the Latin word gratus, meaning "pleasing, thankful". Both of these tools promote thoughts and feelings of appreciation and have similar positive responses. They train the mind and emotions to disconnect and shift into a different orientation to your situation. They both actively promote a self-empowerment perspective through these types of declarations.

2. **Humor:** Humor is all about the quality of being amusing, as well as being a mood or state of mind. It is able to take a more light-hearted view of the circumstances. There are multiple applications with humor that have the capability to seismically change, modify, and shift your moods and perspectives.

3. **Reframing:** This tool is about the practice of assessing a situation, thought, or feeling from another point of view. It provides a framework—literally—to positively reprogram your brain. It is about rewriting the story you are currently telling yourself.

4. **Compassion & Forgiveness:** Self-compassion is about being your own best friend by extending kindness to yourself, especially in instances of perceived inadequacy. Self-forgiveness allows you to focus your decisions to release any feelings of resentment or vengeance towards yourself.

5. **Meditation:** Meditation is a technique designed with the intention to encourage one's heightened state of both awareness and focused attention. This is a widely known consciousness-changing practice. Medical studies show it to have a range of benefits on psychological, emotional, and physical well-being.

6. **Centering:** This technique is widely practiced in the martial arts Aikido and Kung Fu. This practice is known for ensuring you remain grounded, calm, and relaxed, especially in stressful situations. It also utilizes better breathing to maintain a clear mind.

7. **Music:** While Music Therapy has been used for years, there are now new domains in neuroscience studies. Used in various forms, it is valued for encouraging you to smile. It can lift your spirits, focus your brain, and calm your senses. Research suggests movement (i.e., dancing, exercising) to music also boosts endorphins—the "feel good" messengers in our bodies.

All of these practices, combined, have saved my life—from sanity to well-being. I now teach them to others. It is always immensely gratifying to hear success stories from my clients through their use of one or many of these tools.

It is my wish, should you ever find yourself seeking ways to refocus, adjust and/or renew your spirits after a traumatic experience, that these tools will help you, too—with your recovery.

Hey, I'll even throw in *"How to Create Your Own Life with a Soundtrack."* – no rehabilitation required.

About KDB

NO-body expects the Spanish Inquisition!
~ Monty Python

KDB (Karmen De Bora) Wheeler was not expecting a stroke to change the trajectory of her Executive and Leadership Coaching business at the beginning of 2021. Starting the new year usually finds most people reinvigorating their efforts to commit to new habits. KDB found herself relying on her most trusted strategies when her life was jolted by a life-threatening medical event. It was these strategies that helped her survive and transform her experience into a more positive and successful outcome.

Encouraged by medical staff, colleagues, and friends alike, KDB was called to use her vivid story-telling skills to rewrite the narrative of recovery. Showcasing the different strategies she used, KDB weaves a captivating story, inspiring and aiding others who are recovering from their own traumatic experiences. Being a *Life Transformation Strategist* is what her coaching is all about now, and *The 7 Most Important Tools For Bouncing Back From Any Traumatic Experience* catalog her daily and weekly practices that are strategically simple, deceptively easy, and mystifyingly gratifying.

You may encounter many defeats, but you must not be defeated. In fact, it may be necessary to encounter the defeats, so you can know who you are, what you can rise from, how you can still come out of it.
~ Maya Angelou

This was one of KDB's favorite quotes during her recovery. Her own professional mantra, "See one, do one, teach one," reminded her that beyond her education, trainings, and professional experience, it was also her personal experiences that she leveraged to best support her clients in transforming their lives. KDB believes in the processes, tools, and models that she coaches, because she has successfully utilized these same strategies to overcome challenges in her own life.

KDB has been coaching executives and leaders in both the public and private sectors over the past decade. Her unique certifications include George Washington University's Center for Excellence in Public Leadership e-Co Executive Leadership Coaching, Barrett Values© Centre Certified CTT Consultant and Leadership Embodiment© certifications, the University of Santa Monica's LM&SCL II certification, and she is an International Coach Federation® certified PCC coach. KDB graduated *magna cum laude* from National-Louis University with a Bachelor of Science in Management.

Contact info:

• 7Tools.kdbw@gmail.com

CHAPTER 13

HOW MY SPINAL CORD INJURY TAUGHT ME THE GREATEST LIFE LESSON: SELF-COMPASSION

BY DR. OLIVIA ONG

What I have come to understand over time is that lots of people are 'paralyzed' and living their life in an invisible wheelchair. They might be stuck in a job they hate, trapped in a loveless marriage, shackled by unfulfilling relationships that are built on the principles of people-pleasing, or caught in any number of other situations that limit their ability to be truly happy and fulfilled.

I was completely unaware that I was trapped in one of those invisible wheelchairs until I found myself having to rely on a real one. Paradoxically, it was the real wheelchair that showed me the way to free myself through self-compassion.

On one fine spring day in 2008, my life changed forever. I was walking to work when a car hit me at high speed. My body was flung into the sky, and as I hovered, like a slow-motion movie, a few thoughts ran through my head.

See, a few years earlier, in my late twenties, I had ticked all the success boxes: I was working as a doctor in a reputable hospital, I was happily married, I had my own house and car, and I had a great network of friends. But in reality, I was not fulfilled. I lacked self-worth.

Why do so many people who appear to have it all lack self-worth?

I was working as a junior doctor in Melbourne, Australia, before my spinal cord injury. In hindsight, it was easy to see I was trapped in a stressful job that did not satisfy me. But I kept pushing through to please everyone, especially my bosses. As a perfectionist, I used to beat myself up for making the tiniest of mistakes. This was the invisible wheelchair that kept me stuck and feeling overwhelmed all the time.

I paid minimal regard to my own needs as I carried out the responsibilities of my job on autopilot, which is the exact opposite of mindfulness. I was walking from ward to ward, looking at charts, hardly making eye contact with the patients, rushing off to organize chest X-rays in Radiology or follow up on test results. There were days where I was so busy, I even gave myself a hard time for needing to use the bathroom. At one stage, I actually wished I could have an indwelling catheter inserted so I wouldn't need to pee. How insane is that?

For many years, I struggled with feeling like I wasn't allowed to ask for help. I had been programmed to work as a lone ranger. One of the unofficial lessons we learned in medical school was that seeking help meant being weak, not capable, and not competent. This training sat very comfortably alongside the fact that I was a perfectionist. Whenever I made a mistake, I would beat myself up with self-judgement on steroids. I might have ticked all the boxes for success on the outside, but on the inside, things looked quite different. I was going through extreme stress and burnout. If they offered awards for understatement, I would definitely win one when I say I was not extending anywhere near enough compassion to do so.

My lone ranger programming made me feel isolated, disconnected, and helpless.

This was exactly how I felt flying through the air after being struck by a 3000-pound vehicle traveling 40 miles per hour. I landed with an earth-shattering thud.

In the days that followed, I received terrible news. I had a spinal cord injury, and I had lost the ability to walk. I was utterly devastated. I was in shock physically, emotionally, mentally, and spiritually.

So then, there I was, a patient on the other side of the healthcare system. And this time, I really did have the catheter I'd wished for. I felt like a pincushion, with drips in my arms and a feeding tube up my nose. I had never felt so vulnerable, so broken, so helpless.

Experiencing the other side of the healthcare system was really good for me, even if it didn't feel that way at the time. The days I spent in the hospital were really difficult. I had surgery, and for the first few months, I was completely unable to move my legs. Even so, I was still not ready to accept I would never walk again. Meanwhile, I felt so vulnerable and helpless that it took all the willpower I had at my disposal not to completely lose hope. Grief and loss engulfed me. Questions kept swirling through my mind – will I ever walk again? Will I ever be a doctor again? Will my husband leave me? Will I ever be able to have kids?

The days following my discharge from hospital were the worst. It felt like the wheelchair was my enemy. I was terribly self-conscious. I felt ashamed and embarrassed. Every pair of eyes from every person I passed cut into my soul with a knife called pity. I also felt like I could sense relief in the people who tried to look away. It was as if they were relieved it wasn't them in the wheelchair. However, it wasn't other people who were the worst – in the ultimate act of self-hate, I blamed myself for the accident.

My self-worth, which was already low, plummeted to the bottom.

I so badly needed to walk again, not only because I wanted to be mobile but because I wanted to have my identity back – even if it was an identity that lacked self-worth.

One day I heard about Project Walk, a center for spinal cord injury recovery in San Diego, United States. At first, I thought that state-of-the-art technology was what was going to help me. But after spending three years there, I learned a far more powerful life lesson: self-compassion.

My experience of learning to walk again was the exact opposite of my life as a junior doctor prior to my spinal cord injury. Instead of being on autopilot, wishing that I had a catheter to not think about going to the bathroom, I had to be mindful of each step I took. Instead of being a lone ranger struggling to seek help, I connected with fellow spinal cord injury survivors. We bonded through our common humanity and our common suffering – that being spinal cord injury. And most importantly, I transformed from a perfectionist, beating myself up for every mistake I made, to accepting myself for who I was.

After three years of spending five hours every day doing physical therapy at Project Walk, I learned to walk again. I was over the moon, and I went back to my job in Australia, happy, enthusiastic, and ready to tackle new challenges.

WHAT IS SELF-COMPASSION?

Dr. Kristin Neff is one of the leading experts in the science of self-compassion. She describes self-compassion through three key pillars: mindfulness, common humanity, and self-acceptance. These were the things that gave me self-worth – not walking again, and definitely not the markers of success I had judged myself by before the accident.

Mindfulness

The aim in pillar one is to acknowledge our pain and suffering and experience our emotions without suppressing them or exaggerating them. The aim is to observe our emotions with mindful awareness, just as they are. This helps us to avoid getting swept up in unhelpful cycles of negative reactivity.

Common humanity

Often, when we are suffering, we feel isolated. It is helpful to recognize that all humans suffer and that we are all imperfect. In this way, we can reframe the narrative and see that, rather than being isolated, we are participating in a shared human experience through suffering.

Self-acceptance

The key is to be kind and gentle with ourselves when we face suffering, whether it manifests through failure, imperfection, or challenges outside our control. It is helpful to accept these things as a normal part of the human experience, rather than fighting against them and becoming angry, frustrated, or self-judgemental.

Research indicates that self-compassion leads to increased productivity. It allows us to remain calm in the face of failure, rejection, and criticism. This means we can experience improved wellbeing and be more productive and successful. Self-compassion also leads to reduced stress as it activates our soothing system, which leads to greater feelings of wellbeing.

Once I started implementing self-compassion in my personal and professional life, I was much less bothered when my boss commented about me not being up-to-date with my knowledge.

All I did was work out what I needed to study to get up to speed. I decided not to be a lone ranger anymore, either. I reached out to my family and close friends for help. I accepted my injury for what it was and accepted myself for just being me. The truth is, even though I am not able to carry my children and run along with them due to my spinal cord injury, self-compassion helped me accept things for what they were and still enjoy being present with my children in every single precious moment.

Basically, I didn't allow having fallen behind a bit to hold me back in any way. The result of this new attitude was that I not only managed to pass my fellowship exams in Rehabilitation Medicine in 2014, but I also went on to pass my fellowship exams in Pain Medicine in 2017. I became a dual-trained qualified Rehabilitation and Pain Medicine Physician in 2018.

I can genuinely congratulate myself now from a place of self-compassion. It was not easy, but I built a beautiful life from something traumatic and sad. By 2018, I started working as a pain physician in a thriving public and private medical practice in Melbourne, Australia, and going home to a rich family life with my thriving three-year-old son, Joseph. I literally rose from the ashes and became a formidable force in the lives of my family and friends. I became much more influential among my medical colleagues, who had learned to respect me all the more for the challenges I had overcome.

Most importantly, I learned to respect myself. I rebuilt my self-worth through self-compassion, and, in the process, I became a much more compassionate doctor. I now inspire my patients to transform their lives from misery and self-loathing to a place of deep self-compassion. This enables them to lead better quality lives, regardless of any illnesses or injuries they might have.

Self-compassion is not limited to helping you heal from medical traumas. Whether you're a corporate person stuck in a 9-to-5 job, a stay-at-home mom juggling homeschooling three kids in the pandemic, a career looking after a disabled loved one, or anyone who feels trapped, burnt-out, overwhelmed, unsupported, or frustrated, self-compassion can help you feel more balanced and fulfilled.

Self-compassion is not passive or self-indulgent. It is an active process that taps into the basic rights around compassion that all humans deserve. Compassion is not something that we have to earn. We have a right to compassion, even when we feel like we don't deserve it, such as when we make a mistake or feel like a particularly undesirable situation is our fault. Human suffering, regardless of the cause, deserves a kind and compassionate response.

I'm going to leave you with a simple self-compassion exercise.

The next time you are unkind to yourself, put your hand on your heart and take three deep breaths. Much like cuddling a newborn baby, this will give you a renewed feeling of warmth and joy. It only takes 10 seconds. But it could save your job, your marriage, or your life.

The sooner we each develop self-compassion, the sooner the world can heal itself.

About Dr. Olivia

Known as the Heart-Centered Doctor, Dr. Olivia Ong is a life and business coach for doctors, resilience leadership consultant, speaker, author, and pain physician with a thriving medical practice in Melbourne, Australia.

After a severe car accident in 2008, when Dr. Ong was told she would never walk again as a paraplegic, she began walking three years later, is about to write her second book, and runs programs helping doctors transform their lives from burnout to brilliance.

Dr. Ong's global mission is to help fellow doctors who are suffering from emotional and physical burnout to discover the benefits of self-compassion – not just for themselves, but for their patients too.

Dr. Ong is incredibly proud of the *Life Transformation for Doctors* program she launched at the beginning of 2021. As a life and business coach for doctors, Dr. Ong helps busy, high-achieving heart-centred doctors avoid burnout and exhaustion and achieve balanced energy and wellbeing. Dr. Ong has developed a 7-step Heart-Centred Method which includes mind, heart, body, internal and external self-care strategies for burnout prevention and recovery to help her clients thrive at work and at home without the burnout.

Her first book is *The Heart-Centeredness of Medicine*, for which Jack Canfield wrote the foreword. Dr. Ong wrote it because she has not only seen and heard about way too many doctors who were on the verge of burnout due to stress and overwork – she has actually been one of them. Dr. Ong is committed to helping doctors find their way back home to their hearts, where they can lead the heart-centred lives they truly deserve.

Dr. Ong speaks about the pandemic fatigue, stress syndrome, and burnout in frontline healthcare workers and how they can utilize self-compassion to overcome burnout. She offers workshops and speaking engagements on burnout, resilience, and compassionate leadership so that doctors can stay in the game longer as compassionate leaders, and leave a positive legacy for upcoming generations of young doctors to benefit from.

Her second book, *Quantum Leap your Life: The 12 keys to go from Burnout to Joy, Fulfillment & Balance* is due out in early 2022.

Dr. Ong has appeared in the media regularly, including *Yahoo Finance, Thrive Global, International Business Times, Australian Business Journal,* Influencive, and *Auspreneur.* Dr. Ong has been a guest on multiple podcasts such as *KevinMD* and *Everyday Medicine.*

Specializing in both Rehabilitation Medicine and Pain Medicine, Dr. Ong has extensive experience in both specialties. She is a professional keynote speaker in the healthcare industry. Through her public and private practice, Dr. Ong empowers her patients with the knowledge and medical and holistic pain management treatments to manage their chronic pain so that they can lead fulfilling lives.

As a pain physician, Dr. Ong sees more than 1000 patients each year in Melbourne, has been married to her husband for 15 years, and has two children, a son aged 6 and a daughter, aged 1.

Connect with Dr. Ong at:
- Website: www.drolivialeeong.com
- LinkedIn: https://www.linkedin.com/in/droliviaong/
- Facebook: https://www.facebook.com/drolivaleeweeong

CHAPTER 14

BRILLIANT IDEA: START UP WITH 500 DOLLARS, END GAME = 1 BILLION

MY CHALLENGE: AGE 59 (WITH ONLY 16 STRONG WORKING YEARS LEFT)

BY JAMIE CONNER

I went to a liberal arts college in Vermont. During the summer break of my graduating year, I heard about a unique job from Sister's boyfriend. It was July 1981, and I had never had a sales job before. In the brilliance of my young mind, I was thrilled to be selling off-priced Stereo equipment for straight commission on the street. The average burnout for salespeople in the company was 60 days. I lasted four years and built an operation in Boston and Chicago.

By the way, I quit college with only one semester left to get the degree. When I told my Mom that I was not going back to school, she asked why with a look of anguish. I said, let me show you: "The cash savings on the table for two months of work was $20,000."

So here I am, at age 59, with a history of challenges and successes that are amazing—experiencing intense problems with bleak outcomes and tremendous success. Business happens in waves, and my waves were 100 feet low and high. With the last 30+ years in the executive space as the president or CEO, I had to ask myself the question:

Am I willing to hit the streets, cold calling day after day, week after week, with no guarantee of success? I needed to be committed to cold calling accounts in search of the clients that would make up the concrete foundation for the next global enterprise. The obvious answer was yes, with a level of knowledge that I had never experienced before. I knew the last 40+ years of tough experiences were training for me to deal with and rise up, to this day.

The first step was to get my head thinking straight. My first thought was to visualize what the end game would look like—the offices, the people, the global enterprise growing like it was alive. I would spend hours each morning drawing out my vision after the morning meditation. That was the fun part—dreaming of what will be, knowing what the result will be, and the fun in creating something great from an idea. To help turn the thoughts into a reality, I would wake up early, run on the beach and record the description of what the company would look and feel like. I did this again, again and again. This practice of repetition started in my early twenty's. It was around 1985, and I bought a paperback to read, *How to Master the Art of Selling* – by Tom Hopkins.

It was amazing to me that many of the techniques that I had learned on the street were written in that book. Even then, in my early business years, I believed the power was not in what you know but what you do with what you know. So, I memorized the Champion's Creed and followed the belief that anything that is important to me should be a natural response through my subconscious. Repetition is the key to that formula. I would practice, drill, and rehearse (PDR) until my subconscious was satisfied. I would do this repetition in front of a mirror, in the car, just before a meeting, and even on the beach running during the Sunrise. On a personal note, I memorized the Champion's Creed in 1985 and can recite it at will today.

> **When it sounds easy, it is time for a reality check.**

The concept was sound: Manufacture a spray foam insulation product that is world-class in its performance. Build an ever-expanding base of happy clients that love doing business with us. Help them build a better business, and the byproduct is loyalty and profits. When it sounds easy, it is time for a reality check.

On day one, we did not have a factory to manufacture the goods; we did not have customers to buy the goods, we did not have a bank or credit line. We did not have investors that believed in the dream. We had a lack of lots of things.

I did have a 'knowing,' a faith so strong that I knew EcoPolySeal would be a successful world-class brand.

> **"Back to the beginning - cold calling on the street."**

I was sitting in my home office daydreaming about the first-class trips to the Orient (87 so far), with limo rides to the hotels. Exotic places, cutting deals and celebration meals, when reality struck. I need to find a client today. My subconscious was telling me to pick up the phone and start calling. Six hours later, I had my first appointment at a job site. It was only a 9-hour drive, and I could be on time if I left now. I continued to call prospects on the way to the meeting and on the way back. This continued month after month with great success.

> **All that has happened, was meant to have happened.**

I have to take a step back in time to 2016. My daughter needed a dependable car to drive in Colorado. I had a Ram 1500 pick-up truck, so I drove it from CT to Denver and let her use it for six months. She had received a CD set from Marianne Williamson (the Course in Miracles), and I listened to the 6 CDs many times during the 2000-mile drive. That was the beginning of my unwavering faith in the Universe, miracles, and God. The sermons of Dr. Norman Vincent Peale (who baptized me) at the Marble Collegiate Church in NYC became a daily practice. Wayne Dyer and others had a daily influence on my thinking and continued search for my purpose in life. I have driven 400,000+ miles since that trip to Colorado visiting clients, listening, and learning as I drive. It was not a coincidence that I grabbed the Course in Miracles CD set to start my late journey into faith. All that has happened was meant to have happened.

Traveling four to five days a week can be a challenge, with 90% of the challenge coming from my thoughts. So, I learned to appreciate all the good in driving 100,000 miles a year visiting clients. I learned to appreciate and be grateful for an empty road early morning (before 5:00 am) and late at night after midnight. I learned to be grateful for the songs of the birds as I drove past a park...for the Sunrise and the Sunset.

There is a sense of peace in traveling down the highway in between the two dotted lines. It is almost as if you are on your special pathway to get to the destination, following your map to your goal.

> **I would get the queasy feeling that said, "Go out there and go to work."**

There were many mornings that I would be organizing my day, working on marketing, reviewing financial statements, and other fun things that are more relaxing to-do's in business. Then I would get this queasy feeling that said, "Get out there and go to work." The voice would add, "You need to make money today."

Then I would ask the question, where am I going to make money today? What is the most important thing to do for the growth of the company today? What is the most important thing to do right now? Then I would do it.

I felt it was time to raise the bar, but I had to deal with a few issues first. I am not a chronic alcoholic, but I did drink every day for about 40 years. Rarely did I get drunk. Knowing that to wake up fresh every day and build a global company that would make a difference, I needed to stop drinking alcohol.

There was also a personal motivation. There were parts of life that I knew I was missing. Waking up before 6 am, feeling great to listen to the birds and exercise, meditating in the wee hours of the day, driving home after a wonderful dinner. (I had someone else drive after two to three glasses of wine.) Being clear without the fog of recovery was the biggest thing. It has been three years of sobriety so far. Life is good.

Mental breakdown.

The average balance of our checking account was in the high six figures. When the market changed, I had doubled up on inventory as cash slowed (not smart). Wednesday was the day, January 6th, that I realized I would not be able to pay the inventory payable invoice on time. We would be short.

It immobilized my brain, sent shockwaves of failure throughout the brain receptors, blocking creativity and joy. I figured that I had 24 hours to cancel material orders and disrupt the relationship or find a way to make it through. The first action item was to have our CFO/CPA team detail a 24-month cash forecast report. The variables changed, so it had to be correct. They said I could squeeze by if I put in additional personal money and improved collections. It was then that I had a glimmer of hope. So, I let it go for a few hours and came back to it with a fresh attitude. When there is a big problem, I need to convince the guy in the mirror first. I need to play out the scenarios like a game of chess until I am 100 percent sure of the outcome. I reprinted the invoices from vendors, reviewed all the dates, and improved collections. I worked with a few key clients and sold some goods, and I put some of my savings back into the company. This took about five hours to accomplish, and in one second, I knew I could make it through. *My brain turned on again. It was a breakthrough.*

I have become a life-student hungry for knowledge. My set of beliefs have been formed from my experiences. For me, reading a book might have a 10% effect on my actions, but incorporating the idea that was in the book will have an 80% to 90% effect on my life. One of my favorite unconventional teachers, Abraham Hicks, says it best, "Words don't teach, experiences teach." I have a three-step habit for my continued improvement:

- One – read, listen, write, review, repeat.
- Two – incorporate in my day right away.
- Three – repeat until it is a natural habit.

Being grateful is not 'pie in the sky' fluff. I believe it is God's gift to all of us. It is a knowing that lives in my heart and soul. When you own being grateful, it is real. As usual, it started with repetition. I have always been grateful for easy stuff, the Sunrise, calm water to water ski on, a beautiful spring day in New England, and a large bonus. It was not until I attended the Tony Robbins' *Date with Destiny* that being grateful became a permanent part of my life. My personal mission statement now includes being grateful, which I have practiced, drilled, and rehearsed until my subconscious owns it.

Jack Canfield came into my life through the *Chicken Soup for the Soul* book that I read flying back from Hong Kong in 1995. Dr. Norman Vincent Peale came into my life as he baptized me and soared back into my life in the 1990s. It took a decade of life for me to be ready to really get what these amazing teachers have been telling me.

I have come to understand and believe that when the student is ready, the teacher will come.

I guide my team to build a global organization that manufactures world-class spray foam insulation—with our end goal of helping to reduce global energy consumption by forty percent. I remain vigilant in being grateful for the challenges, opportunities, people, and relationships in my life.

Never, Never, Never give up on your dreams!

- Author's note: All dates are approximate and reflect my personal beliefs based on what I have learned and experienced throughout my life. I have no intention to copy, infringe or quote from any publication.

About Jamie

Jamie Conner is an American author, motivational catalyst, corporate turnaround specialist, and entrepreneur. Jamie is the co-founder of Fun Source LLC, Source Manufacturing LLC, and North American Spray Foam Polymers, LLC. He has served as the CEO for startups to global enterprises, with travels that brought him to make just under 100 business trips to East Asia, Europe, South and Central America. He is regarded as an expert in international business, marketing, sales, leadership, and motivation.

Conner was born in New York on May 29th, 1959. He spent his teen years in Syosset and Shelter Island, New York. With only one semester left to graduate from Goddard College in Vermont, he devoted his life to business. He became a lifelong student with his focus on business, behavior, and motivation. He is a co-author of *Success for the Soul - Vol. 3*, with leading author Jack Canfield (author of *Chicken Soup for the Soul* Series).

Conner started his working career as a young teenager of 14 in a neighborhood retail lighting store. Enjoying hard work with a curiosity for how people interact, Conner was introduced to sales in 1980 during a summer job. He became a legend in the retail industry and held positions as Salesman, Sales Manager, VP of Sales, President, and CEO. He is regarded as an expert in the Housewares, Personal Care, and Construction industries.

Conner loves water sports with a special affection for water skiing and footing on a calm lake. Outdoor activities in nature at the top of his list include bike riding, running, hiking, and snow skiing.

Contact information:
    Jamie Conner – Vero Beach, FL
* Email: JC@jamieconnerlive.com

CHAPTER 15

CONSCIOUS PARENTING FOR THE TWENTY-FIRST CENTURY

BY JORGE FRANCIS CASSIR, MD

To be the best possible parent is a joyful experience. It will make you feel alive, energized, and fulfilled. The conception of a child generates a torrent of love from your heart that you share with your spouse *and* your child, binding you all in an indestructible bond.

If you are a woman planning to get pregnant, be ready to be the gardener of the most beautiful garden you will ever know—your own womb, where your baby will germinate as an expression of love in which the parents and the baby become one. The happiness your baby brings will last a lifetime. Your intention will become your reality; such is the power you possess. You can create a family based on love, happiness, and trust, wherein everyone feels heard and respected. This is how your baby can grow with serenity, peace, and self-confidence. The universe has brought you to this point of parenthood, and it has your back! It will provide abundantly for a prosperous future if you believe in it, visualize it with intention, and work toward its realization.

Please express gratitude for the abundance in your life, no matter how little materially it appears. Life is a miracle to be appreciated with reverence; and the universe has created you with a purpose that is for you to discover with introspection aided by your intuition, your heart, and your soul. You will never run out of the free air you need to live in the moment because the universe provides it abundantly. Similarly, if you have laser-focused intention and live with the perspective that life is bountiful, you will receive the material abundance that you deserve.

Traditional religions worldwide support the rising belief that human beings are both physical and spiritual beings. Accordingly, the teachings in this chapter are spiritual, free of religious dogma. Today, human beings are so distracted by the materialism of a world with rapid technological advances, especially in the social-media platforms, that they ignore the spiritual essence of our being. That's why we see stress overwhelming even children, exacerbated by the Covid pandemic; even high-school and college students face stress with mental-health issues that overwhelm facilities. We need parents who are prepared to practice a new form of parenting that utilizes a new operating system. Introducing that system is the intention of these pages.

To understand this new form of parenting, it is helpful to explain what I mean by the words *conscious* and *unconscious*. A conscious person seeks to live according to his or her spiritual purpose guided by the Higher Self. The values of compassion, fairness, generosity, humility, and forgiveness are prominent. An *unconscious* person, in contrast, lives blindly in accordance with the small self, preoccupied with financial success and materialistic values. This preoccupation naturally breeds fears of lack, envy, greed, self-doubt, grandiosity, and the tendency to control, manipulate, and lie. But while such characteristics are in the service of self-interest, they are actually *self-limiting* in that they keep us from developing to our full potential as human beings. And if being unconscious limits our own potential, it also limits the potential of our children.

An integral part of my teaching is to help parents increase their own consciousness in order to rear conscious children who will be able to protect themselves against the fears and self-limiting beliefs that for centuries have crippled most of humanity. This threat is largely invisible, because we are silenced by a vague sense of shame and an unwillingness or inability to understand the scope of the misery it produces. My dream is that parents and grandparents everywhere will bring their own wisdom to ameliorate this peril to the human race through caring for their own children and expanding awareness of the problem.

So, other than striving to live consciously, how do we begin to prepare to be the best parents possible? Deep in the heart. Once there, parents may imagine the baby they themselves were when they arrived on this planet. If they were to describe themselves as they were then, they might use such words as *innocent, trusting, vulnerable, living in the present, always happy, never needing to go anywhere, fearless, curious, never hurrying, never demanding, nonjudgmental, loving, tender, liking to be held, having a sense of rhythm, loving to dance, responding to lullabies, and always smiling at the sight of their parents or siblings.*

Thinking of themselves as grownups, though, these same parents would likely describe themselves in words *opposite* to those above, such as *controlling, fearful, unhappy, judgmental,* and *calculating.* How could they have grown up in a loving family and gone to "good" schools only to make such a wrong turn? The answer is that they did nothing wrong except follow the rules of the well-intentioned but mostly unconscious institutions—and I include the family and society at large in that description.

The problem is that societies throughout the world have gotten it mostly wrong. Consequently, shortly after birth children become filled with untold fears, and the problem only gets worse as the years go on. Our schools put children in boxes geared to measure results in the cognitive aspects of mathematics and science and less in creative and emotional pursuits. IQ testing in the United

States may not reveal the intrinsic gifts that children may have. Competition for grades causes anxiety and may stimulate lack of confidence so that the child does not claim an ability she harbors in her heart. Yet such intrinsic abilities may produce greatness beyond the educational system to instill. How could we teach a child to be a Nelson Mandela, or a Gandhi, or a Martin Luther King, or a Mother Theresa? We cannot!

We all know people who enjoy showing off and building themselves up. These people are very insecure. Whether they need to control others or every part of their business, the trait exhausts them. Instead of planning a secure future with confidence, they spent a lot of time and energy listening to their inner negative voices. These voices reside in the amygdala, a small part of our brain that processes the emotional responses such as fear, anxiety, and aggression that torment most of us. The amygdala is the home of the ego, the part of the reactive brain that developed the "fight-or-flight" response to danger as part of our early evolution when we were often attacked by predators. In modern life it is less useful; still, we must express gratitude to it for being there to help us in crunch times. Befriend it and assure it that you have control of the situation. Please refrain from battling it, because, as depth psychologist C. G. Jung said, "What you resist persists."

Negative emotions rapidly solidify into beliefs, or the acceptance that something is true without proof. Each of us has a long laundry list of negative beliefs. I invite you to take a few minutes and write your own list.

Then the best way to deal with these negative emotions/beliefs is to turn the tables on them and express the opposite emotion—I call it "ego flipping." It is good to practice this technique for yourself in order to clear your shadow before connecting with your child to be conceived. For instance, if your emotion is one of lack, flip it to the opposite and think of abundance. If the emotion is one of unhappiness, think of happiness. If you are frustrated, express gratitude. When imagining the birth of your fragile, new baby, you may fear that you will be an unworthy parent and will make harmful mistakes. Flip that emotion by assuring yourself that you are indeed worthy—not only because you will be mindful in nurturing a healthy child in love and joy, but also because, in willing to become a conscious parent, you are responding to a call from your soul. And then you can pass this meaning on to the spirit of your child if you are called to do so.

Being aware of this maneuver of "ego flipping" is important so that you can deal with your fears and self-doubts effectively. If you have a deep-rooted problem, consider seeking professional help. When you become a parent, it is important not to plant your own fears into your child.

To aid in my own healing from negative emotions, I add to my daily meditation an "Inner Child Meditation" (ICM). I imagine being my inner child—vulnerable, innocent, accepting, and trusting—and feeling that I am one with all that is. I visualize divine Light coming into my mind and body and intentionally aim it toward an issue that needs healing attention. Then I ask for guidance about the next steps. And the guidance comes! I repeat the ICM three times a day as part of a short meditation, not lasting more than three to five minutes.

Now that we have discussed how to deal with negative emotions and easing the pain they cause, you can begin preparing for your baby's conception in practical ways:

(1) Plan for childcare. Do you and your spouse both work? If so, do the employers allow one of the parents to stay home for a while with your baby? Can you *afford* to remain at home for an indefinite amount of time or to hire a nanny? Or can you rely on another family member?

(2) See your family physician and treat your medical issues. Select your OB–GYN and midwife if you are interested in having your child at home.

(3) Eat organic foods and take supplements and vitamins as your medical team advises.

(4) Exercise using moderation; use light weights to work your muscle tone.

In addition to seeing to these practical matters, also begin to think about instilling values in and disciplining your future child. Do you and your spouse agree? Bear in mind it is best to let the baby unfold from within, the same way that a rose does. The way to rear your child is by allowing him or her just to be.

Having prepared in the above ways, now you can best invoke conception. Even when your child is still just a thought, you as future parents can dance with her or him, talk with her, ask him if he needs anything. And you can meditate. Every morning, meditate for five or ten minutes, allowing more time if you can, to connect with the soul of your baby-to-be. This way you can connect from your own soul and reassure your baby's soul that she will be accepted and loved as she is, that you will always be there for her unconditionally. Meditation based on deep love will increase the chance of a successful conception, pregnancy, and delivery for both parents and the future child.

Also, prepare a *ritual* for your baby's conception. I suggest making this ritual a celebration of your baby's creation—as both a physical and a spiritual experience. Light scented candles and meditate with your spouse to connect your souls with the soul of your baby. Then have a cleansing bath or shower during which you and your spouse embrace and kiss, at once as an act of love and in celebration of the divine miracle of creation. Feel the reverence and awe of this moment! Then retire to your love nest and release the magic. Ignite your passion and allow it to set off the fireworks! This is how I recommend the conception of a child should be.

Body and soul are inextricably intertwined. The body is the soul's temple. Both are an expression of the divine energy of creation; both are essential for experiencing life as human beings. Likewise, both Mother Earth and Father Sun—"our paradise"—are essential to all life. Heaven is not out there but deep within each of us! Understanding this concept is a wonderful way to welcome a child and important to teach him as he grows up. Encourage her to observe nature along with you and to hear nature expressing itself in silence. Explain that life unfolds like the miracle it—and she—is: from the inside out. Once we are born, we all have our life journey, and we must allow our children to fall and get up as many times as required to fulfill their destiny, just as we do.

About Dr. Jorge

Jorge Francis Cassir, MD, was born in Colombia, South America, to a Colombian mother and an Egyptian father. His father's addiction to gambling led to a breakup, as his mother did not want to trust the family's future to a gambling table. The author was about eight years old when his mother decided to separate and took her two children with her.

When the author was about eleven, he promised himself that, if he ever married, he would be there for his children all his life. At twelve, he discovered and was inspired by the French physician, philosopher, humanitarian, writer, theologian, and organist, Dr. Albert Schweitzer, who was doing missionary work in Africa.

By the age of thirteen, Jorge had the intuition that his most significant work would come late in life. At about the same time he heard the word *enlightenment* but did not know what it meant. But he liked the sound of it and told himself that he, too, would like to be enlightened one day.

When he was eighteen, he learned via a long-distance phone call that his father had taken his own life. Jorge felt nothing, since their separation had already amounted to a metaphorical and emotional death. Little did he know that his father had developed his gambling addiction within his own family of origin, as his people had been casino owners. The year that his father was born, the family lost a significant part of their fortune and developed the belief that the baby was "bad luck." Thus, his father grew up as a wounded child.

Inspired by Dr. Schweitzer, and with his mother's support, Jorge became a physician. He was unaware at the time that he had chosen the life of a healer—first of bodies suffering from cancer, which he treated with radiation, and then in response to a calling to heal potential and actual families both emotionally and spiritually. Dr. Cassir has been happily married for fifty years. With his wife he has reared two happy children who have made their parents proud as they enjoy the wonder and love of their four grandchildren.

It should also be noted that Dr. Cassir will be listed in the prestigious roster of Influencers, Marquis Who's Who for 2022.

Contact information:
- Website : www.IntentionalConception.com

CHAPTER 16

FAITH: THE GREATEST SUPERPOWER IN YOUR ARSENAL FOR SUCCESS

BY MERCEDES S. DAUPHINAIS

Optimism is the faith that leads to achievement.
Nothing can be done without hope and confidence.
~ Hellen Keller

Who am I?

… Just a girl who followed a dream to Los Angeles.

What's the line from Pretty Woman?

…*"This is Hollywood, land of dreams. Some dreams come true,*
some don't, but keep on dreamin'."

I lived my California dream. It was 100% promise and potential.
It was sheer sunshine that came crashing down into indescribable
physical pain, three years of homelessness in LaLa Land, and
more than a decade of dependency on crutches. I went from
working in customer service and management for a major
corporation to sleeping in the back seat of my Prius, praying
nobody would notice I was there.

Things got really real in my world, but that's a story for another time.

I had my own personal legion of earth angels watching out for me and helping when they could; still, it was challenge upon obstacle upon brick wall. Beyond *"What happened?"* the most common question was, *"How are you smiling? / How do you stay so positive?"* I don't want to mislead anyone. There were a couple days I was a ball of tears literally brought low on the floor, and plenty moments of epic frustration. But overall, I really did smile, stay positive, and live in the certainty that this misery would only be for a season.

Let me ask you a question. What do you believe in? So you know where I'm coming from, I believe in the God of the Bible. But this isn't that kind of *faith* conversation.

-- Do you believe in God?
-- Do you believe in a friendly universe and a brighter tomorrow?
-- Do you believe in humanity?
-- Do you believe in your ability to get scrappy and figure it out, whatever **it** may be?

Faith far outweighs so much, and it doesn't have to be the same flavor as mine to work. Though, in all transparency, I do believe my particular brand of faith offered an extra measure of resilience, peace, and endurance; but we're here to discuss faith available to all walks of life.

Faith is an access to courage, to stepping up and doing whatever there is to do, no matter what you're facing down. Faith is the superpower that gave me the fortitude to endure craziness with confidence for tomorrow and greater grace than the situation would typically allow, especially over such an extended period of time.

Dreadful days happen, they're part of life. Sadness, frustration, and anger are all elements of the human experience. But, if we're willing to really live the moments and extract maximum value from those experiences, we can leverage them to strengthen our belief muscle and do our faith reps. That's when the action required to shift the narrative becomes a whole lot easier.

Whatever you're up to, whatever the next mountain to climb – good, bad, or ugly – the strategy applies.

I would acknowledge that when you're able to leverage the faith to overcome any challenging moment (fleeting or prolonged), that is, in itself, its own success. Declare victory! The same practice employed over time can be a supercharged, souped-up, superpower entree to whatever form of success you're after. Set your sights with precision. Plot your course. Have faith. Put one foot in front of the other. Persist. Persevere. Soar.

I can hear you thinking, *"Well, that's all fine and dandy, but... how?"*

I'd like to share some of the strategies that made it possible to keep a right mind in the midst of insanity, to walk in faith and emerge smiling, to have a clear vision of the start and finish, and to declare victory after victory along the way within the greater race.

First is being thankful in all things, places, times, circumstances, and in every storm. And, yes, that's Biblical – both in origin and potential. Gratitude practices have become so commonplace that if you're anything like me, they may elicit an internal eye roll. But here's the deal, they work.

Practicing being grateful to the point of making a practice of being grateful can shift the very foundation of your life.

Sometimes I need to start with something as basic as: *thank you for the air in my lungs, that I woke up this morning, for the food in my belly, that my heart is beating.* Some days that's what it takes, and that's okay.

While you're at it, acknowledge yourself! What did you do well? What results did you get? When you open yourself to hear, your inner voice will know what thanks to offer up. Things get really interesting when you're authentically grateful for the storms, the challenges, and the obstacles as well. It's all about reframing.

Worry and anxiety rob us of faith. In the face of stress and overwhelm, when faith seems absent or fear creeps in, a deep breath and a few sincere offerings of thanks can change the whole equation. Speaking of breath, breathing is an access to belief. Breath can bring you back to center in moments of frustration, anger, and distress. Breathing deeply and intentionally can turn the world on its axis, create a polar flip, and turn that frown upside down. It can be as simple as paying attention to the air entering and exiting your body.

Whether it's faith in yourself to handle the next critical task or project, or your belief that circumstances will align to get you to the other side with style, grace, fireworks, and maybe even a few champagne corks; *the moment we allow ourselves to dance with despair, our access to faith is wholly stymied.* Thoughtful moments of gratitude and breathing can be extraordinarily useful, whether in a moment of overwhelm or not. Practice makes progress.

Speaking of thoughts! We know our beliefs are the result of persistent thought, yes? In that sense, we get to choose. Becoming a ringmaster able to tame the roaring lions of unbridled thought in the three-ring circus of the mind when we have yet to begin can seem a beastly task, maybe even impossible. I promise you it's not. If you want to shape your beliefs, and therefore your faith, thought management is key...and, it's absolutely doable.

A friend recently shared a story of his children and how he has diligently worked to instill in them, *"You become what you think about."* Wisdom!

I have another wise counselor who penned similar words long ago, *"For as he thinketh in his heart, so is he..."* (Proverbs 23:7, KJV). Although Proverbs is most often credited to King Solomon, some scholars believe this chapter of wisdom literature may have gleaned influence from Egyptian philosophy more ancient yet.

There's nothing new under the sun, least of all what we're discussing here. However, it can be a turning point to encounter ideas from a new perspective or a different person. I hope this is such a moment for you.

Researchers have discovered there are certain things we can be aware of that allow us to seriously uplevel our game. The training I've had in peak performance coaching leads us to these next few nuggets:

1. **When we think bigger, the number and scope of actions available to us expand.** So, think BIG! SUPER BIG!! GINORMOUS!!! Then, take action and generate results. Faith in your vision, the bigger the better, is critical to productive behavior.

   Still, don't be intimidated or feel like your faith must always be huge. Remember what my main man, J.C., said as well, mustard seed-sized faith can move mountains. Sometimes a little is all you need. Yet, intention and persistence in growing our faith and the ways and the contexts in which we are able to apply it expands our impact in the world.

   Happy little side effect? Sell yourself, and you'll sell the world as well. Not everyone, not all the time, but it completely changes the game, especially internally.

2. **A little success grows our faith in our ability to get results.** Stepping up, stepping out, finding courage, and being bold to take action and achieve an outcome is what expands faith in self and the capacity to bring a vision to life.

It's an ever-expanding cycle when initiated and sustained.

Greater faith leads to action, which leads to results. Results lead to elevated faith in whatever you're up to, *greater* action, and *bigger* results. And on and on it goes. We absolutely want repetition of experience when it comes to this. We want those ever-expanding circles.

When we master and leverage this expansive cyclical tool of *belief* → *action* → *results* → *bigger belief* → *bigger action* → *bigger results* over time, the extraordinary becomes possible. If Einstein was right when he said, *"Compound interest is the eighth wonder of the world,"* imagine what this kind of compounding can generate in your life.

3. **Powerful growth mindset** *(Carol Dweck)* **and internal locus of control** *(Julian Rotter)* **are gamechangers.**

Growth mindset primarily involves…

- persisting through and embracing challenges
- trying new things
- knowing failure is part of the process, fertilizer for growth
- the certainty that attitude and effort determine abilities
- willingness to receive and apply constructive criticism

An internal locus of control means believing you dictate the happenings and happiness of your life, versus being a victim of circumstance. Life is going to happen to us on occasion, some things are out of our control, but we still get to choose where we stand. This is particularly critical to remember when we encounter obstacles, doubt, or balloon deflation of any kind. Have faith that you get to determine your own fate, and you do.

There are all manner of ways we can shore up the foundation of our lives to reinforce access to powerful faith in people, the world, who we are, who we're able to be, and the difference we can make.

- Develop awareness
- Choose love of self, others, and creation
- Dream, cast vision, take action, and stand powerfully
- Choose to know failure and being wrong are part of the journey

More time in nature, less with screens. Very little on earth brings us back to a powerful headspace and solid footing faster than fresh air, vitamin D, and a few positive ions.

Good people. Travel in remarkable circles. My *Band of Merry Misfits*, one of my remarkable circles, gathers most Sundays to live and laugh. They are priceless and beyond precious to me. Find joy in your people and what you do. Play!

Power of choice in belief can shift the same physiological sensory experience of fear, nervousness, or anxiety to one of excitement. It simply comes down to choice, and faith in where you stand in the universe. One intentional mental shift has the capacity to fundamentally transform our posture in the world. Next time those experiences arise, be willing to take a moment, take a breath, and choose to redefine the physical experience as giddy excitement. You'll be amazed. It really does work.

If we funnel all of these observations and techniques into an expanding, closed loop system, it allows us to master our thought-life, strengthen our faith, and show up in all-new ways on entirely different levels.

Einstein posited, *"The answer we find determines what we do with our lives. If the universe is a friendly place, we will spend our time building bridges... We decide."*

Do you have faith in a friendly universe? Are you ready to be a bridge-builder between where you stand now and where you want to be? Do you have faith in yourself, in others, in the world, in your vision? We get to choose.

You are capable of the extraordinary, perhaps even what some might consider impossible. The most readily accessible foundation to the bridge that will get you from here to there is faith. I believe in you.

Breath. Thoughts. Gratitude. Optimism. Vision. Choice. Hope. Confidence. Belief. Faith. Action. Persistence. These things do a merry maypole dance in our lives. When well leveraged, they can launch us to the stars.

Step it out, over and over, day after day, moment by moment. Engage in every interaction with the bearing of one who is and does and has all you want to be and do and have, and something inexplicable happens. Reach for being a tiny bit better with each passing day. According to researcher Steven Kotler, 4% seems to be the ideal target. Do it week after week, year after year. Do the things you know to do, and you will witness miracles.

And do remember to celebrate the victories. A willingness to celebrate progress, large and small, is vital. It can make such a difference in our mindset and reinforce the faith we have for each next level as it arises. Not to mention, it's fun! Be willing to have fun and enjoy it all.

With these tools (and a wonderfully loving community), I watched life go from homeless hot mess and more than a decade on crutches, to business owner who has learned to walk again, step by step.

I can't wait to see where it all grows next.

Do give yourself grace and patience when you don't happen to have outrageously powerful faith and/or excitement. It's a practice that takes practice. You'll get there as long as you persist in faith and action.

Oh, and please choose to keep the tough moments as brief as

possible. Life is a rollercoaster, but we have much greater control over our experience than we tend to allow ourselves to believe. Will you endure the ride with your hands over your eyes? Or will you throw your arms high, laugh with abandon, and enjoy every twist and turn and loop, whatever the silver lining or shining moment?

With faith as the foundation, by taking action day after day, and growing the compound interest of you, you will know success beyond your wildest imagination. When those particular dominos start to fall, you'll begin to notice cause and effect in ever-increasing measure. The inner giddy happy dance that ensues is something you must experience for yourself.

One final secret. Sometimes the incredible machine between our ears forgets that the cause is, in fact, the cause of the effect. We develop an odd amnesia and think it's no big deal to eat the proverbial doughnut. When we develop the discipline to do the small things, the tasks and habits that point in the right direction again and again over time, even when it seems unimportant, we begin to see incredible results. When those outcomes appear to have come out of nowhere, I implore you to remember that they do, in fact, come from somewhere. They come from the tiny powerful choices. Keep doing the little things you know serve the larger outcomes you're after. They are connected.

I can't wait to hear about your moments. I can't wait for you to have commonplace, seemingly miraculous breakthroughs. Personify authentic faith, and you have a very real superpower in your arsenal for success.

I have faith. I believe.

YOU CAN DO THIS!

To your success!

About Mercedes

A Rocky Mountain girl through and through, peak performance coach, writer, speaker, and creative artist, **Mercedes S. Dauphinais** is a graduate of the University of Colorado at Boulder, with a B.S. in Business Administration, a B.A. in Professional Spanish, and a certificate in International Business.

Despite having truly enjoyed seven years of working for a major corporation, Mercedes went off globe-trotting and dream-chasing. The consequential life implosion provided the perfect prescribed burn to grow a whole new crop of faith-based purpose-driven efforts.

On a direct path to a life beyond the footlights, a bizarre accident put an end to performance (and even walking) for more than a decade. The return journey from that particular detour provided invaluable lessons, insights, and a whole new *raison d'être.*

More than 20-years ago, Mercedes discovered a voracious curiosity when it comes to the machinations of the brain and the tendencies of the human animal. Maybe her Psych 101 professor was right, perhaps psychology would have been the natural path.

Mercedes trained in both theoretical and practical coaching techniques to help others *bring about positive, permanent shifts in the areas that matter to them with power, freedom, and full self-expression.*

In 2011, she became a certified LENS Neurofeedback practitioner and has been a ruthless student of personal development and human behavior longer yet.

Having spent ten years in transcontinental tri-generational deep daily Bible study, guided by the wisdom of her mother and grandmother, she now has a vision to craft tools to serve Jesus-lovers in their pursuit of whole-life development and peak performance, that all would one day come before the Father and hear, *"Well done."*

As of the publication of *Soul of Success, Vol. 3*, Mercedes is collaborating with some of the leading research scientists in peak performance and flow to develop a Christian-minded training program. The goal is to merge what has been gleaned from human observation through science and culture and weave it together with ancient Biblical wisdom. To nest what man has perceived inside of what God has been whispering to our souls from the beginning of time, with an aim to help believers elevate their lives to the next level and beyond, is her *why*.

Mercedes is the creator of **Praiseworthy Goods** (whose purpose is to bring smiles, inspiration, and Scripture to the world through physical products) and **Mustard Seed Moxie** (through which she and her team are committed to providing practical tools for and walking alongside motivated people of faith, focused on living as the powerful child of God they were created to be.)

Though it may not be possible to offer a steaming mug and a front porch swing, if you're curious to connect and know more, pop by! The team would love to *"see"* your smiling face.

www.PraiseworthyGoods.com
www.MustardSeedMoxie.com

And, if you'd like to stay in touch, join the email list.

One final note from Mercedes & her team:
"May the Good Lord bless you always... in all ways."

CHAPTER 17

THE RESET BUTTON
RECLAIM YOUR POWER AND TRANSFORM YOUR LIFE WITH "SEVEN TOOLS" TO FEEL FANTASTIC AND LIVE THE LIFE YOU DESERVE!

BY VALERIE WHETSTONE

What is success? I feel it is not measured by the position that one has reached in life but by the "obstacles one has overcome" and the actual courage to take a step forward to achieve greatness!

Even when there is nothing left, and I'm down to my last breath,
I'm not giving up! No, Not Me!
~ Andy Grammar

Andy Grammar's song, *Don't Give Up On Me*, sums up my life. For over a decade, I have been in a health crisis searching for answers, and I have encountered hundreds of closed doors on my journey of life. I felt abandoned, frustrated, scared, anxious, and left in horrific pain with no vision for how my life would turn around. I was financially strapped with medical bills, my family and friends didn't know what to do or say, I was forced to completely give up my career as a teacher, mom, and child education advocate. My life was looking pretty grim. However, by facing the dark night of my soul, reaching depths unimaginable, I reached my hands and heart out to my higher power and found my "true self." My story is one of will, determination, and courage to face the unknown. It is called **"FAITH!"**

My life was perfect! I was a teacher, mom, child education advocate, married to my high school sweetheart for 30 years, and blessed with two amazing sons. I exercised daily, ate healthy, and took care of myself on the outside, but neglected my inner self. I have always been an overachiever, which was fine for most of my life. I thought if I worked hard, I would succeed. This philosophy was working until I truly burnt the candle at both ends. My health took a drastic turn for the worse. I was extremely fatigued from adrenal burn-out. I had digestive issues, hormonal issues, migraines, plus extreme pain from pelvic prolapse.

I decided to have a hysterectomy and fix my pelvic prolapse. This decision has forever impacted my life, for the complications from pelvic mesh have been unsurmountable. Ten days after my surgery, I started hemorrhaging, blood pouring out of my body down my legs like I had just exploded. I was passing large chicken-breasts-sized blood clots and was rushed to the ER. I was scared, confused, in intense pain, and fighting for my life. I made a promise to God as I was rushed into the operating room, if he saved my life, I would forever be grateful and would serve him. This near-death experience was the "wake-up call" I needed because I was clearly going in the wrong direction. I had ignored the warning signs my body had been trying to give me, but this time I had no choice but to listen.

Thank God I was breathing, but the obstacles I now faced seemed unsurpassable. Undergoing four surgeries in two years, I was left with severe pain and neurological issues from surgical complications and pelvic mesh. At one point, I was unable to even lift my arm, feed myself, or have the strength to open my eyes.

I became paralyzed in my right leg, had severe pain from nerve damage in my pelvis, back and legs, lost control of my bladder and bowel, and experienced daily seizures. I had to be carried everywhere because I couldn't walk. I wasn't able to talk to my friends or family for more than a few minutes due to extreme fatigue. My brain literally felt like it had been scrambled. I was literally shut off from my world into one of darkness. To top it off, I now had gauze coming out in my stool, apparently left from one of my surgeries. Seriously, What else could go wrong? I was living a true nightmare!

However, deep down, I still had an inner strength and persisted to seek answers. I attended doctor's appointments daily and endured over five years of poking, probing, closed doors, no answers, no sleep, and severe pain beyond what anyone should ever have to experience. The trauma and emotions of **frustration, stress, worry, anxiety,** and **fear** became a true reality. I had no more energy to give, I was completely splattered. I had literally become "spilt milk!" I remember asking God one night, am I going to die? My body was getting weaker and weaker, and the pain was excruciating. I was mad that I wasn't going to be able to serve him. One night I remember staring at the ceiling with tears rolling down my face, curled up in my pink, cozy blanket at 3 a.m., praying for God's mercy. It was then I made a decision to take back my life and take action. I didn't know the how, but I knew I wasn't going through all this s--t for nothing!

Piece by piece, I collected "ME!" I started reclaiming my power and collecting all of my broken pieces. I had to find a way to literally create a new persona, a new life, and leave the past behind me. It took years of research, going back to school – taking classes online, listening to every audiobook about self-help, healing, PTSD, trauma, pain, and spirituality. I spent every waking hour, which was all night long, doing whatever I could to propel myself forward. I truly awakened my giant within!

I was making progress, but it was slow. My best decision was to invest in my own life. I found a mentor to support me. It was the catalyst for my emotional growth and healing, as well as it opened the door to new possibilities and more prosperous ways of being. What I discovered was a set of tools that worked when identified, assimilated, and applied with consistency and persistence. These tools took me from being a "victim" to a "victoire."

I love this quote by Howard Thurman, "Don't ask what the world needs. Ask what makes you come alive and go do it. Because what the world needs is people who have come alive."

I now have an ignited passion for helping others transform their lives. I became the founder of *Doorway To Transformation*, a certified Transformational Life Coach, Dream Builder® Coach, Mind-Body Wellness expert, a motivational speaker, a master of Emotional Freedom specializing in EFT, a master of Energy Medicine specializing in the Energy Codes, a Spiritual Coach, Mindset/Visualization Tools Expert, and I co-authored a Best Selling book, *SHORT, SWEET AND SACRED.*

It is my honor to share with you the most valuable insights, processes, and tools I have gathered through my own personal journey and in coaching and mentoring my clients. It is time to ***RELEASE, REPROGRAM, RECREATE and RENEW!***

Reclaim your power and transform your life with "seven tools" to feel fantastic and live the life you deserve!

RELEASE

Time to clear out the crap in your life.
Erase the limiting belief that it is "hard" – it will be if you think it is!

TOOL #1: Everyone's favorite...Val's "*Uck it Buck it"

Write down your **"old story"/negative thoughts** on a piece of paper.

Be sure to include how it makes you **FEEL**?

1.

2.

3.

Example: Life is overwhelming. I feel stuck, angry, and frustrated.

Next, write down your **"new story"/positive thoughts** on another piece of paper.

1.

2.

3.

*Use the words *"I AM"* to add **power** to your statement.

Example: I am a good sleeper. I feel so fantastic when I wake up rested each day.

(Save the "I AM" statements, you will use these in tool #4)

Now crumple up the "old story" and put it in the bucket or trash can, for it helps symbolize the action of letting go.

Once the bucket is full, put the papers in the garbage, or burn the papers and release them to the Universe. Just make sure to burn your papers safely! (I almost burnt down my house because I threw the papers away while the embers were still smouldering, and my trash can started smoking!!! My son had to quickly throw the trash can into the pool! LOL)

Do this practice daily, weekly, monthly until you get the results you want.

TOOL #2: Get rid of physical clutter in your life!

When you decide to "let go," you create new space for something better to enter into your life.

For nine days straight, give away, throw away, or eliminate 27 items! (This sounds crazy, I know, but it is possible. I remember thinking how in the world can I get rid of 27 items in one day?) If you miss a day, you have to start all over because the energy is cumulative. *No Cheating!* You will be surprised how **energized** you will feel if you follow the directions completely.

Ideas: clothes, shoes, old medicines, broken pens, pencils, dried-up markers, delete old emails, anything that brings you an unpleasant memory or binds you to the past.

. . .It's time to move on!

RECREATE

TOOL #3: Create a "VISION" for your life.

Ask Yourself:
1. Where are you right **now**?
2. What do you **want**? Where do you want to **go**? What does your life look like three years from now?
3. **Why** do you want it? (When your purpose is powerful, you will do whatever it takes to achieve your goal!)
4. What **steps** can you take to achieve it?

The biggest mistake I see with my clients is they are "wishy-washy." To create anything in your life, you must eliminate your excuses, make a **clear decision**, and **take action**! If you require the support of a mentor to get a crystal clear vision for your life, I would be blessed to work with you, so you can start living the life you deserve! **I believe in YOU!**

REPROGRAM

TOOL #4: Affirmations

Affirmations help you create the reality you want by reprogramming the subconscious mind to encourage you to believe certain things about yourself or about the world. At first, it feels like you are lying to yourself, but by repeating your affirmations, you will start to believe it. You will act differently and see life from a new perspective. (Use the list of "I am" statements that you created from above.) Say each affirmation out loud in the mirror every day.

Example: I am of vibrant wellness!

TOOL #5: Visualization

If we want to manifest anything in our lives, seeing it clearly in our minds helps anchor the feeling in the body. Research shows that the mind can't distinguish between what is real and something imagined, so the mind begins creating new neural pathways based on whatever it is we are imagining.

Journal: Write in the present tense as if it already happened!

SEE IT! FEEL IT! CREATE IT!

Example: Today, my family and I hiked the Mist Trail. It felt so incredible with each and every step I took, enthusiastically moving forward in my life. As I reached the top of the waterfall, I felt so empowered and completely FREE!

Vision Board: Use a poster board to create a collage of whatever inspires YOU. Be creative using photographs, magazine cutouts, affirmations, inspirational words, quotes that represent or symbolize the feelings, possessions, and experiences you want to attract in your life. Look at them daily to prompt yourself to visualize your ideal life on a regular basis. Imagine them as if they have already come true. This is one of the best ways to activate the Law of Attraction. Think about including a picture of yourself, one that was taken in a happy moment. Have fun!

Example: Jordin Sparks, winner of American Idol 2007, cut out a picture of herself and glued it on the front cover of *Entertainment*

Weekly along with the words, "American Idol 2007 Jordin Sparks" before she even made it to the Top 10.

RENEW

TOOL #6: Self-Love

Mirror Exercise – A powerful technique for increasing belief in yourself. Every morning and night, look at yourself and smile in the mirror. Give yourself a hug and say, **"I love you!"** (It might feel silly at first, but trust me, it works.)

In order to promote your own mental and physical health, do a conscious act to take care of YOU! Ensure you get enough sleep each night, take time to get some fresh air daily, eat healthy, or partake in a hobby.

TOOL #7: Present Moment Reminder

Be present. It is a gift you get to open each day!

Too often, we get stuck in our heads, living either in the past or in the future. This just amplifies worry, fear, and frustrations.

1) Use my acronym **STOP** – "Surrender Time Out Please!" to help you become aware of your thoughts. You must physically stop and notice what you are noticing.
2) Re-pattern your thoughts...Think of a new story that brings you joy, peace, or whatever "feeling" you want. **Visualize it!**
3) Take in a breath...like you are smelling an apple pie,
4) Breathe out...like you are fogging up a mirror.
5) Set an alarm to remind yourself three times a day to physically **STOP** what you are doing, notice what you are noticing, recalibrate and **breathe**.

Now when you go back into the world, you can approach life with a calm, centered, and empowered place.

BONUS: Gratitude

Start each morning with a hand on your heart and thank GOD, the Universe, or whatever you believe in, and be thankful for your breath. I know that some days you may feel stuck or frustrated. Gratitude is the closest thing you have to a "cure-all" magic fix for anything in life. It shifts your energy instantly. I suggest writing in a journal each day.

Example: I am so happy and grateful now that...

Unfortunately, we all face struggles at some point on our journey, but it is what you do during the challenges that truly changes your trajectory in life. I still have mountains to climb, but I am confident I **will** surpass them all! Remember if you think you can, you will. Baby steps!

I truly believe that we are greater than any circumstance! Make the shift from simply surviving to actually thriving financially, emotionally, physically, and spiritually.

On the mirror in my bathroom, it says, *If you believe in yourself, anything is possible!* Even when my life looked grim, I truly believed that I would bounce back, and so can **YOU!**

It is time to **RISE** and take back your power. You don't have to do it alone. I will teach you how to overcome any circumstance or condition in your life, increase your confidence and gain clarity by guiding and supporting you on your journey to transform your life.

About Valerie

Valerie Whetstone resides in San Jose, CA and is a leader in transformation and empowerment. She is truly a beam of light to all who are lucky to encounter her. She is the founder of *Doorway To Transformation*, a certified Transformational Life Coach, Dream Builder® Coach, teacher, Mind-Body Wellness expert, a highly sought-after motivational speaker, co-author of the Best Seller – *SHORT, SWEET AND SACRED*, a master of Emotional Freedom specializing in EFT, a master of Energy Medicine specializing in the Energy Codes, a Spiritual Coach, Mindset/Visualization Tools expert, and best known as the "*Uck it Buck it" girl.

Valerie is an enormous inspiration to everyone who knows her. She focuses on client-care excellence with the same level of passion and love she gives to her two amazing sons and husband of 30 years. Valerie is active, engaged, and present in everything she does. Her true passion is helping others transform their lives to feel more vibrant and confident. Her mission is to inspire, motivate and empower you to live the life you deserve. She strives to give you HOPE, for you are born to shine!

Valerie guides clients to realize their true potential and power by re-patterning their current belief systems. She provides a proven and reliable system that brings the RESULTS you are looking for in your life. She offers various coaching programs to give you a variety of tools, tips, and resources to help you break through and become more confident, empowered, and abundant in all areas of your life. Valerie continues to prove that we are all capable of overcoming any circumstance, condition, or obstacle!

She believes in integrity and lives what she teaches. Faced with devastating news, Valerie had a choice to give up or reclaim back her power and live life fully. Her own journey of pain and health obstacles has led her to want to help others feel supported, loved, and encouraged to become and reach their highest self.

It is her personal attention, a desire to always advocate for and do what is best for her clients that has made her a loved and sought-after life coach and speaker. She loves engaging with people and hearing their stories, helping them turn their dreams into reality. Through her retreats, meditations, workshops, and cutting-edge programs, she strives to meet her client's needs in every aspect.

Valerie's personality radiates as she is able to connect with your audience. Valerie's high energy will inspire, entertain, and deliver a message that is dynamic, impactful, and fun. Valerie uses the power of story to help her audience reclaim their power and ignite the fire of their dreams.

When she's not managing her business, she enjoys being in nature, doing pilates, spending time with her family and friends, traveling, tending to her garden, and celebrating wellness, a positive mindset, and spirituality.

If you would like to work with Valerie or invite her to speak, please visit her website:

www.Doorwaytotransformation.com

[The "*Uck it Buck it" — available for purchase on her website.]

Or contact her at :
- Val@doorwaytotransformation.com
- Facebook: Doorway To Transformation
- LinkedIn: Valerie Whetstone

CHAPTER 18

ALL ABOUT THE EFFORT

BY SHANNON FAULKNER

Shoot for the moon. Even if you miss, you'll land among the stars.
– Oscar Wilde

I'm looking around at my colleagues to see if their facial expressions are showing the same punch-in-the-gut feeling I have. I think they just look shocked. Me too. The news we have just been told is that our employer, a dream company really, is moving. And they are moving far. With their words, they did share that our jobs were safe and how it was going to be exciting to join the other part of the business with a bigger site to bring us all together. What I heard, though, is my three-hour daily commute has just turned to four. On a good traffic day. Five more likely.

Now for some people, the move was actually closer to where they were living, and they were quite happy with this new company adventure. For me, having two young children and supporting all three of us on a single income, this was going to be now a further stretch with extra childcare costs and fuel for the tank. So financially, this was going to hurt, but more importantly, it was the extra time away from my boys. Trying to fit the fun family time after work was now going to be impossible, and this was going to hurt the most. So, less time, less money, less freedom.

191

My world now officially sucked.

Going home that evening with a heavy heart, I tucked the kids into bed and pulled out my calculator. It was time to see the truth about this move. This wasn't the first time I did a budget, of course, and I knew how much disposable income I had to dip into for these extra costs. So off I started—Mortgage, Utilities, Taxes, Rates, School Fees, Car Costs, Food, Childcare, etc. And now to also include the extra fuel costs and additional two hours of childcare? Ouch. That hurts. So, if I decided not to go on any family breaks, not to buy the occasional ice-cream treat for the boys, and switch to the cheap walk-in hairdresser, the boys and I would just make it. Not an ideal situation, though.

I knew that something had to change, and I knew what the answer was, but I really didn't want to admit it to myself. Doing the latest budget and searching similar roles on my laptop showed that there was a ceiling to the amount of income that I could make. An important realisation was that working for another company meant that I was not in complete control of the location of the work, no further amount of money could be earned quickly, and no control over the days that I could be with my boys. So again, time, money, and freedom felt out of my control.

Then this hit me like a ton of metaphorical bricks. I was selling my time and freedom for money. Wow. I had never thought of that before. Now, this realisation brought something else. I could do anything. I remembered as a child how I thought of life as unlimited possibilities. A seed was now germinating in my mind, and I knew it would grow quickly with action. I needed to take some serious action for the life I visualised for my boys and me. And I knew I couldn't do this alone.

When you are an employee and looking to leave a company, it is a tricky situation. You don't want the word to get out that you are planning to leave, and at the same time, you need to get the word out that you want to leave. These are the times you look through the Rolodex of friends, colleagues, and associates that you know you can trust. But just before you do, you may consider a vacation!

I had already booked to go to the south of France with the kids to one of those holiday family resorts that have lots of gooey ice cream bubbling on the hot pavement and the screams of children laughing in the pool that can be heard for miles around. My boys were in heaven. The Mediterranean Sea was quite near, but one had to drive to get there, so off we went with piles of sand buckets and sunscreen taking up any available space in the car.

We settled into a sandy space with the warm sea in front of us and walked into the water to cool down. It wasn't long before my oldest had already met some new friends to play with, and as I was wading with my little one in the water, I heard a friendly voice from England asking if it was my son who had befriended hers. Now, this was not just a chance encounter. This was serendipity with the Universe delivering to its finest. I had just met a soon-to-be lifelong friend and my very first business consultant.

Nic was not only a business consultant but worked for one of the major players in the industry for several years. She was currently on maternity leave and not planning to go back. The only time she was going to share her knowledge, she said, was with her own consultancy. There was no fear with Nic. She knew her value and what she had to offer to the world.

Jumping out on one's own, I had considered. My best friend owned his own business, and advising him always felt purposeful. There remained one thing in the back of my mind, though. Imposter Syndrome. Like really, who would have wanted my industry knowledge and then pay me for it? Well, as it turns out, lots of people. My best friend was the one who first told me so. And to this day, I am ever so grateful for his belief in me.

When I got back to England, I set out a plan. First, I recognised that I am now going to own my new title, Business Consultant, and secondly, going to figure out what the heck a Business Consultant does to make a living at it. I needed some help, and I knew who I could trust on the path to getting to my new destination – Jo.

Jo and I were due to meet up shortly anyhow. We are not only business colleagues in the industry but also have become good friends over the years. She was well connected and thought of very highly by all. I knew I could trust her, and it was the best thing I did. Her wise advice to me was to get out there, have as much exposure as possible, and connect with those that can help me on my next journey. She introduced me to other consultants over coffee, got me invites to networking events, and even seats at formal black-tie dinners. My world of opportunity had opened, and I was receiving it with open arms.

Now going to these events was one thing, but the effort from me was still needed. I was still in the first year of my company location move, and with the additional travel hours, it gave me a lot of thinking time to consider my options. Should I join a consultancy firm and have them bill me out to other companies? Should I try and make it on my own under my own brand? Should I partner with someone else? And of course, the dreaded question, am I going to be a success at it?

As these questions rolled around in my mind, I continued to show my presence at as many events as possible, including getting up on stage and speaking about my area of expertise. Going up there and presenting filled me with fear every time. Would I trip up the stairs walking on? Would my mouth become so dry that I wouldn't be able to speak? Could everyone else hear the beating of my loud-drumming heart? Does anyone want to hear what I'm saying? And so much more. And yes, it was every time. And yes, I kept going back for more. My key motivating factor, the one that said make the effort and get out there, girl, was knowing that it would only take one opportunity to fulfil my goal. The one goal is to be in full control of my time, money, and freedom.

Along the way, I met quite a number of loving villains. You know the kind that care deeply and love you but have the ability to freeze you in your own tracks and try to guide you down the path of least resistance. The path that is safe and warm where you can keep doing what you are doing, and no one judges; they may even encourage you to stay there! As I opened up to more people around me, I did find these loving villains surrounding me and sometimes even convincing myself they were right.

And then I remembered something that I had heard years before: Look to see from whom the advice is coming. Have these people made the effort to stretch themselves to reach their goals? Were they in a financially successful space? Did they have an abundance of time and freedom of choice in their daily lives? As I remembered, each person who gave me their advice, I asked myself these same questions above. When the answer was no, I thanked them for their love and concern, then let their advice go.

While driving the commute, I started to see businesses I drove by differently. From the small corner store selling everyday needs to the large corporate office with their name emblazoned to be seen for miles around, I now saw there was one person who made that company happen. Whether these businesses succeed or fail may be up to many. The start though was with the one. This one person had a vision and took a leap of faith in themselves. The success came with the first step of opening the door or convincing others in their dream of greatness to build the empire. I knew right there and then that I wanted to be *The One*.

When a person decides to take full responsibility for themselves and starts actioning this belief, it is amazing what opportunities start to open in their life.

Over a year after the company announcement, I got the call. It was from a small but established company that was looking to grow financially, operationally, and with more leaders. And they wanted me to lead this charge. The owner had heard me speaking on stage a few weeks earlier, and after consulting with his team, they decided they wanted me. Yes, me. There were two matters, though, that needed to be dealt with. One, I was still employed. Two, this company wanted to employ me – a good problem to have if you are leaving your employment for another, not a good problem when your vision is to spread your wings and work for yourself.

What I had learned on my journey up to this point is that the only one who can take away my dreams is me. Deciding to be fully responsible for my time, money, and freedom was now non-negotiable. I contacted back the owner of the small company and gave him my return offer. I would be willing to come and lead his project, the non-moving part though, it would be on a consultancy basis. He agreed! It was also important that I stated my other terms of business, including weekly time spent on the project and financial compensation. These matters were all successfully agreed upon between us.

When I went back to my then employer and told them that I would be leaving for pastures new, it was done with such confidence and gratitude for the opportunities they had given me. By the time that I left, it had been two years since the announcement of the company location move. During those two years, I had put in so much effort to grow and learn not only about myself but the value that I could share and give to others.

It has now been five years since leaving my corporate world behind. I have continued to grow and develop myself during this time to share more knowledge with my clients. From having a hat-trick of co-authoring three books, being selected as a judge for the Women in Credit Awards four years running, to becoming a certified Canfield Train the Trainer and a certified Business Coach—just to name a few opportunities that have opened up for me and I am truly grateful.

So, if you would like to know how you can enhance making the effort to your own success, here are a few steps you can take:

1. Make a list of everything you're an expert on or passionate about professionally. Decide what you want to focus on from your list and set your goal to get there.

2. Find a mentor or coach who has been where you are and can help transition you to where you want to be.

3. Put yourself out there. Join a mastermind, find networking groups, attend conferences, or link into social media groups talking about your subject, or anywhere else! Just get out there.

4. "You are the average of the five people you spend the most time with." – Jim Rohn. Go hang out with people you aspire to be like and become the average of them.

5. Aim to tell everyone you know, and even practice on those you don't, where you are aiming to go. It's amazing how many people will want to help you get there.

It's all about the effort.

About Shannon

Shannon Faulkner has been advising and consulting for over 20 years in the financial services industry, where she has successfully executed projects in operational department start-ups, rebuilt company customer experiences, and increased business efficiencies for clients who are Fortune 500, Top 100 Best Employers, and Market Disruptors.

How has she helped her clients become so successful? By not knowing that she couldn't be successful and then instilling this belief in them. She also runs her own company called TheBluDoor as a certified Business and Success coach catering specifically to business owners, leaders, and entrepreneurs.

She is a member of many industry associations and partnerships, including Mindvalley, BMSU, and Wellnomics.

One of her testimonials reads:

My experience working with Shannon Faulkner has been life-changing. Shannon is a coach that uses both her personal development skills as well as her business acumen and network of individuals to improve the lives and businesses of others. In my case, she was able to make an introduction that translated into me personally earning over $1 million USD for my business. I highly recommend Shannon to anybody who wants to get to the next level in life and in business.

-Melissa J Shea
CEO, Everyday Realty Holdings

Learn more about Shannon and her services at:
- www.TheBluDoor.com

CHAPTER 19

WHAT YOU GIVE, YOU GET BACK
IDEAS FOR HELPING OTHERS

BY PHILIP WALTER SMITH

I have a very simple mission for my life:

Help people build assets, create jobs, and raise their standard of living.

I learned a long time ago that if I can help others, my financial rewards will always be greater than what I expected. My clients and friends made money from my guidance and assistance. Those clients and friends then came back to me for more assistance. As a result, my income multiplied because I helped them.

WHATEVER YOU GIVE, YOU WILL GET BACK!

You may help someone today and nothing happens for years. But then, all of a sudden, that person may be back in your life and helping You in some way. Let me give you an example of how someone will come back into your life and help YOU. In 1995 and 1996, I went to Kazakhstan as a volunteer to work with a bank on their conversion from the old Soviet system of bookkeeping to international accounting standards. I was there two times and presented classes during each visit.

The banking sector in Central Asia was changing rapidly after the dissolution of the Soviet Union. The bank had hired an English consultant named Martin to assist them in the operational and budgeting issues facing the bank. We became friends and spent a good amount of time together sharing ideas of how to restructure the bank. Some of those conclusions became part of his overall plan at the bank. He was very grateful for my assistance.

Now fast forward to 2002 to Kabul, Afghanistan. I had been hired by the British government to introduce accounting standards (International Financial Reporting Standards, or IFRS) to the central bank of Afghanistan. One day we were requested to attend a meeting at the US Embassy about a US-sponsored project that was to begin to assist the central bank in their regulatory, supervision, and accounting functions. When I walked into the meeting, the hostess was my former boss from the United States Agency for International Development (USAID) in Moscow. Sitting next to her was my friend Martin from Kazakhstan.

The lady proceeded to tell us the US was going to be doing the work, and they would no longer need any of the British people to assist the central bank. If that were to be the case, my work would be finished, and my contract would be cancelled. She asked what I was doing, and I told her my portion of the work was the introduction of IFRS. She advised me I would no longer be needed along with the other advisors.

Martin immediately spoke up and took exception to her statement. He said very simply he had worked with me in the past and knew of no one else who could do that portion of the project as well as I could do it. He suggested I be allowed to stay and complete my work while they would use the funding for the IFRS instructor elsewhere in their budget.

And that is exactly what happened. My work continued for several months. The point of this recollection is to show *you* if *YOU* do something for someone without expecting anything in return, your actions will be rewarded in the future in some way. The consulting fees I earned were almost $100,000 for the period I stayed in Kabul.

When I was in Afghanistan in 2003, I asked my interpreter if he knew a family that could use some help. He asked, "Why?" I told him I just wanted to do something to help a family. The next day he said he found someone whose family could use some help. It happened to be the family of one of the women who worked for us as a house cleaner.

Her husband, father, and uncle had been killed by the insurgents in Kabul. She now lived with her children, her mother, another uncle, and several cousins. They had a nice house, but it had no electricity. It was easy to help them. We bought a large generator, gas cans, electrical fixtures, light bulbs, and five hundred feet of electrical cable so they could install the electricity into the rooms where they wanted it.

We made arrangements to deliver the materials. As is the custom, it was imperative we visit with them to have some tea and refreshments. We knew the custom, so we brought several kinds of tea and several bags of fruits, nuts, and other groceries. They expressed their thanks, and we went on our way.

The real surprise came the next day. The woman who worked for us thought my actions were meant as an expression of interest in her to be my wife! Her mother and uncle had met me when we were having tea and had already given their respective approvals. She told my interpreter she agreed, and we could be married as soon as I was ready.

After getting over that shock, we immediately told her marriage was not my intention. My only intention was I wanted to help them in their current living situation. And I had no strings attached to my actions. Fortunately, our local driver was also interested in this woman. He was very jealous of me for my actions to help the family. We also assured him there was no other interest except to help them. He then proposed to her to become his fourth wife within a few days.

This is just an example of doing something to help others with no strings attached. The lesson I did learn was I needed to be careful of the potential repercussions of my actions in each culture where I wanted to help. One of my experiences in Afghanistan was with a lady who worked as a cosmetology expert for weddings. At an Afghan wedding, all of the ladies in the wedding party are made up with detailed sena paintings on their hands, arms, and faces. This lady worked for a salon that offered the service.

My translator knew her family. She was living in a one-room apartment with her two children, plus her sister and her husband and two children. My wife and I talked with her about starting her own business so she could raise her standard of living. She wanted to find a better place to live and wanted to send her children to school.

Together we came up with a business plan that involved a loan to her of $1,200. We agreed to interest of ten percent per year, and the total plus interest would be paid at the end of one year. We signed an agreement.

A year later, she came back to us and wanted to pay us. Her business was growing, and she had her own salon. There were five chairs in the salon where ladies could be made up for weddings. Seven people were working full time. And she lived upstairs with her family. Both of the children were going to school. And both of the children had their own bedrooms.

She handed an envelope to me for the repayment. We told her we did not want to be repaid. But what we wanted her to do was to find someone who had a dream to start their own business and make a loan to them. And when they come back at the end of the year, do not accept the repayment. Ask them to find someone with a dream and use the funds to help them get started.

Over a period of years, I followed the money. I did several projects in the country from 2002 to 2017. The lady with the salon helped me keep track of the money. Her business continued to grow, and her children finished high school.

The help each time when the repayment was due worked five times. According to the lady with the salon, the sixth business was demolished when a car bomb exploded in front of the business. The best part was the five businesses where it did work had about fifty people working. That would mean a good number of families are benefiting from this plan. And it all started with the original $1,200.

Did I benefit? Yes. The company with which I worked in Afghanistan knew what I had done. They saw the results. And they called me back for more consulting. There were at least four separate assignments, and I earned tens of thousands of dollars in fees from each assignment.

Money? A smile? Your time to help them? Give what You have. You will get it back multiplied. Every time You do something for others, You will be planting another seed. Those seeds will grow. You need to know how to give. Generosity takes some training.

Who will You give the money to? You will get different results from different people. Start with those who need it. They may appreciate it more and can certainly use the help. There have been times when I just wanted to do something nice, and I was rewarded well as a result. There is one recollection I will share with You.

My boss, who was worth hundreds of millions of dollars, was

always accompanied to lunch by someone. The people with whom he was having lunch always expected him to pay for lunch. I invited him and his wife to dinner with the condition that he would let me pay. On the following Saturday, we went to his favorite restaurant and had a lovely evening.

The next day he invited my wife and me to go on a day-long trip with several stops along the way. We had a lovely brunch overlooking the ocean at the Shawmut Inn in Kennebunkport, Maine. We then drove to his old high school in New Hampshire and had a spectacular dinner with one of his former classmates who owned a local restaurant. He refused to allow me to pay for anything. At the end of the trip, he made one comment to me. "No one has offered to buy me dinner for decades. Your act of kindness will never be forgotten." I paid for his dinner, and it came back to me multiplied.

There have been other examples like that. *My experience shows that once YOU do something like that on your own, without the help of anyone else, it will always come back to YOU in a favorable way.*

When *YOU* are deciding who should receive the money, try to find someone who is already helping others. Why? Because when *YOU* help them, it will have a wider effect on more people. And it will multiply the effect back to *YOU.*

The following is an example of how I helped one lady build her business that eventually supported many families. In May 1995, I did my first volunteer assignment in Bishkek, Kyrgyzstan. My interpreter and I talked about helping someone who was already in business to find a way to help them grow. She knew one lady who she thought would be a good candidate.

A meeting was arranged with the interpreter, me, and the lady. Her business was making "national things" which were sold in the local bazaars as souvenirs. She showed me some samples, and I thought the work was very neat, clean, and well done. She explained to me she worked with her mother in a small room where they lived. All the sewing was done by hand.

I asked how much she could do if she had a new sewing machine to do the work. She thought they could make four or five times more of the products for sale. We made a deal. I would give her the money to buy a sewing machine, and she would give me samples of all the various products. I got a large bag of those "national things" which I shared with my friends and family in California.

I did another volunteer assignment in Bishkek in 1996. I met my interpreter, and we visited the lady and her mother. They were doing well enough with the sale of their products to be able to buy a second sewing machine. And they now had four people working making the products and two people selling the products.

In 2004 I was back in Bishkek for a different project. I organized a follow-up meeting with the lady. She now had her own building with twenty sewing machines and forty people working in the building. They had eight people at four different locations selling the products.

In Kyrgyzstan, there are about four people per household. If forty-eight are working, the total effect would be on almost two hundred people. I was very pleased with the result. There were no strings attached with this lady. She did exactly as I hoped she would. She made a difference and helped others.

My personal declaration has been I will give twenty percent of every bit of income that comes into my possession. That is off the top before any expenses. So, if I have a salary of 1,000, the first 200 is allocated for charity. Period. No exceptions. I have been doing this for a while and I feel good about it. I have already helped dozens of families. Every time I can complete an action to spend the 20%, I feel very good about it.

It is better if *YOU* are going to be giving the money to someone who will be working for it. You may have an office. It needs to be cleaned every week. Why not hire someone who needs help to come in and clean your office? You will be paying someone to clean it; why not a person who really needs it?

Another example I would like to share with You is my experience in Ghana. My driver lives with a woman who was taking classes as a seamstress. When she finished the classes and received her diploma, she worked out her apprentice arrangement and was ready to open her own shop.

I knew they did not have very much money. The cost of a good commercial sewing machine was researched. I made an agreement with the lady. I would buy the sewing machine, and she would make things for me. In addition, because I needed someone to do ironing and alterations because I had lost some weight, she would be able to spend some time in those areas.

We agreed on the amount she would be credited for each hour she worked for me or for the time she spent making things for me. I would deduct the hourly amount from the cost of the sewing machine.

I told her it didn't matter how long it took for her to reduce the balance. We agreed the most important thing was her ability to start up her own little business so she would have a decent standard of living in the future.

About Philip

Philip W. Smith was born in Cumberland, Maryland, in 1945. He has published several fiction and non-fiction books. As an international finance expert, he has worked with the banking sectors in thirteen countries. More than 13,000 have attended his seminars in the last forty years.

Phil has been described as sensitive, kind, intelligent, well educated, quick-witted, and well-read. He has travelled to 57 countries and lived in more than a dozen countries while trying to understand their cultures. His legacy is helping people, especially small businesses, who can grow and create employment for others.

The companies he has helped now employ more than 3,000 people. With a quick temper for incompetence and ignorant people, he is also self-critical of himself. He is obsessive in his quest to be the best in everything he does!

Phil made the following list that shows his personal commitment to giving:

1. I died three times and came back stronger than before.
2. The near-death experience made me realize I needed to take control of my life.
3. I did take control of my mind, my body (I lost 95 pounds), and my levels of stress (I now have almost none).
4. I can show the audience the method I used to eliminate 99% of my stress.
5. I lost my eyesight in one eye in Iraq. Our convoy was attacked by snipers, and during the action, my retina was detached. I didn't know it until too late, and the retina could not be re-attached.
6. Recovering from the eye operations led to the writing of my first book. (Thanks to an incredible drug I was given for pain relief.)
7. My latest book, *YOU ARE THE MOST IMPORTANT: THE ROAD TO EVERYTHING YOU WANT IN LIFE*, was written while in quarantine in May 2020. The book is a guideline for anyone who wants to change their life. And it reinforces the benefits received when you do something to help others. The book and e-book are available on Amazon and Barnes & Noble. It is being sold in Kyrgyzstan (Russian language) and in Ghana and the US (English language).

8. I am now married to a wonderful, intelligent, strong, and beautiful woman who also happens to be a doctor/surgeon. In 1998, as a nurse, she assisted in the operation during which I died twice. She was also there when I saw the white lights four days later. She knew me first from the inside out! Now, as a doctor, she can take care of me for the next 40 years.
9. By taking control of all phases of my life, including loving myself, believing in myself, and trusting myself, I am now the happiest man in the world.
10. I have now committed to giving 20% of all gross receipts from my businesses to charity. We have already distributed tens of thousands of dollars and hope to be above six figures in 2021.

For more information about our programs and books:
- Company Website: www.philipwaltersmith.com
- Facebook: Philip Walter Smith, and group PHILIPWALTERSMITH
- YouTube: PhilipWalterSmith
- Instagram: philipwaltersmith
- Email: PhilipWalterSmith@gmail.com
- Email: philipwsmith@hotmail.com